ACCEPTABLE INEQUALITIES

ACCEPTABLE
INEQUALITIES

AN ESSAY ON THE DISTRIBUTION
OF INCOME

BY

IAN BOWEN

Professor of Economics, University of Western Australia

London
GEORGE ALLEN AND UNWIN LTD

FIRST PUBLISHED IN 1970

© *George Allen & Unwin Ltd 1970*

SBN 04 330161 4

PRINTED IN GREAT BRITAIN
in 12 on 13 pt Fournier type
BY T & A CONSTABLE LTD
EDINBURGH

PREFACE

There is at present no agreed policy at international level about inequalities of wealth and income. There is not even much clear thinking on the kinds of inequality that are to be tolerated, and the kinds that ought to be remedied.

This book attempts to reopen a discussion on the question of objectives. There will probably never be unanimity, nor even a wide consensus of opinion, on these problems, but if attempts can be made to clarify what each of us thinks, at the very least we may be able to identify our points of difference.

This is only a beginning. As I wrote the book, I found that the issues of policy raised had many ramifications. Since the world's division into poor and rich nations is not only marked, but likely to get even more extreme, and since inside both the poorest and richest nations there are socially dangerous extremes of fortune, the subject is surely worthy of a general airing. Out of discussions such as this, perhaps clearer thinking, and ultimately more effective policies, may emerge.

Here is a summary of the nine chapters that follow.

Chapter 1: *Present Discontents*
This discusses the present widespread disillusion with political and social arrangements, and the principles, or lack of them that they seem to embody. Ultimately this is a protest, however confused and incoherent, against manifest inequality either in wealth, status or power.

Chapter 2: *Minimum Practicable Inequality*
Is there perhaps some range of inequalities, rather than an un-realizable ideal of egalitarianism, that can be set up as a practical objective? This is a theme first mentioned here, and returned to in Chapter 9 especially.

Chapter 3: *Education and Inequality*
The classical liberal remedy for inequality is a massive dose of education. There is an inherent contradiction in this idea since, for groups, education promotes distinctions and divisions, as well as, for individuals, narrowing gaps and opening up opportunities.

Chapter 4: *Forces in Society that Promote Equality*
Some economic forces too work for greater economic equality in society as well as for rising average real incomes. Other economic pressures can be identified that strongly promote greater inequalities.

Chapter 5: *Inequality and Politics*
Poverty, and other aspects of inequality, are not economic questions only. To reduce inequality political action is necessary; to give is to exercise power. The American anti-poverty campaign, and the 1960s programmes of international aid, provide striking case studies of this.

Chapter 6: *Ethics and Economics of Redistribution*
Giving within nations or between nations is often advocated as morally desirable, but what exactly are the principles on which gifts ought to be based? Who morally owes whom how much?

Chapter 7: *Inequality and Developing Economies*
Some of these (India for example) started out after independence with extreme egalitarian goals. These have tended to become modified as problems and internal contradictions mounted up. An important connexion seems to be emerging between the internal and external problems of inequality so far as these economies are concerned.

Chapter 8: *Income Determination*
How should relative wages, salaries and property earnings be fixed? This issue has long perplexed industrial relations experts, and practising politicians in many countries. Are some principles

8

now emerging, and perhaps some concept of an acceptable inequality?

Chapter 9: Acceptable Inequality
Will inequality increase? There may yet be conflicts within societies, but these may become less sharp if certain reasonable consequences of the existing divisions are accepted. A revolutionary but acceptable solution is possible, but not unless its outline can be first defined.

CONTENTS

CHAPTER 1

THE PRESENT DISCONTENTS

Our present troubles, whatever else they are, must surely be described as social and economic. They are conditioned by history and sharpened by geography. But the quarrels between groups are not only the heritage of past events, nor are they determined by the places in which people live. These provide the setting and the colour of the conflicts now in outbreak or seething beneath the surface of a temporary accommodation. The conflicts themselves are an aspect of present society.

As this is so, social scientists should be the persons most appropriately trained to understand what is going on, to interpret actions, to provide a critique for ideologies, to analyse the performance of groups in relation to their expressed or implicit goals, and above all to predict what may happen in the future. Yet the literature of the social scientists is not yet famous for expressing all that might be expected from it. The interpretations are often obscure or irrelevant, the critiques shallow, the analyses pedantic and the predictions false.

This is not to condemn the social sciences as useless. Like all sciences, their practitioners include pedants and traditionalists. In science there has to be much dross for every ounce of gold. Methods evolved to analyse statistics or to measure the distribution of income, have become sophisticated, and are nowadays better fitted to describe the society and its economy than were those available thirty years ago. The problem has been interpretation and judgment, not sources of information as such, much though these could be improved. How should the economic evolution of society be interpreted?

One family of explanations was directly descended from Marxism, and comprised the various versions of communism. To those who were not dedicated party members, most of these explanations seemed inadequate. They were insufficiently linked with the facts, alleging exploitation where none or little existed, and predicting increasing misery for workers in capitalist countries despite their rising real incomes per head. An alternative to the Communist Manifesto was offered by W. W. Rostow, who substituted rising mass consumption for the era of beneficent socialism predicted by Marx. Unfortunately Rostow's ideal was not much more attractive than Marx's, and his analysis of past economic events, though plausible, could easily be shown to have little merit as an account of past industrial revolutions. His predictions, however, were influential, since his thinking deeply influenced successive Americans in high places.

The Rostovian view of the world was like this: all national economies could be treated as entities. An economy was not really progressing until it had passed a discontinuous 'take-off' phase, after which it experienced 'self-sustained' growth, presumably requiring no further assistance or stimulus from the rest of the world. All economies could be classified under this scheme according to the stage that each had reached, and this necessarily implied that all had much the same ambitions and goals, namely the mass-consumption society.

This was essentially the ideology of a stage of American power consciousness, that culminated in 1960 in John F. Kennedy's election. There was a strong ingredient of American idealism both in the diagnosis and in the prescriptions for economic aid to developing countries that logically followed. Enough aid must be given to give a 'big push' so as to start a national economy on its self-propelling upward path.

Weaknesses in the analysis were the implied neglect of the effects through international economic relations of one economy on another, and the neglect, too, of the growth of administered prices within the manufacturing world, and the pressure on the terms of trade of organized advanced industry against the competitive primary sectors in many underdeveloped economies. There was a cultural weakness in the belief that all economic ambition could be summarized in the ambition to become a mass-consumption society.

Consistent with the Rostovian view of the world, which flourished at the end of the 1950-60 decade, was the optimistic belief that liberal democracies would govern the ever-increasing number of ex-colonial territories which, according to American idealism, should be freed from the various old imperial yokes as quickly as possible. The only exception was to be for territories acquired by the United States, and this was on the grounds then still seriously argued by American officials, that the United States, because of its eighteenth-century record, was above the suspicion of imperialism in 1960. The new nations would of course need considerable economic assistance in their early stages (pre 'take-off'), and, therefore the 1960s were to be the 'development decade', the turning point in history.

Shallow, facile and incorrect though this analysis seemed to be to most international planners and statesmen outside the hot-house of Washington, there was no strong motive for many to oppose it. After all, if the American Government and people chose to bemuse themselves with an ideology that seemed to be consistent with small-town oratory on July 4th, that was to a large extent their own affair. Their anti-colonial bias led to policies that agreed well enough in practice with communist thinking on the same issues, although the left-wing analysis was quite different from the American, and equally wrong. As for the middle powers, the old colonialists like Britain, France and Portugal, the first two were convinced by the most realistic evidence that the days of the old imperial systems were gone. New forces throughout the world, nationalistic and vigorous, had to be accommodated and acknowledged. Contacts between the older industrialized countries and the newly emerging coun-tries had to be put on a new basis, economically and politically.

Everyone therefore went along with the American theory, whether accepting it or not. But in the 1960s it was shown by events, as well as by arguments, to be gravely deficient. The newly emerging economies wanted to go their own way politically, regardless of American wishes, and curiously indifferent to American claims to be totally anti-imperialist. American power was deployed throughout the world to 'contain' first the USSR and then Red China, on lines that had been politically designed by John F. Dulles, but in Vietnam there were signs of resistance that led to the instability and overthrow of the American-sponsored Diem Government.

So it came about that the 1960s, instead of becoming a decade of peaceful take-off, became a decade of guerrilla wars, of revolutionary and counter-revolutionary coups. Not only in Vietnam, where the situation worsened and the extent of military operations became far greater than anyone in 1960 would have been prepared to predict, but in Indonesia, in the Indian sub-continent, in Nigeria and in the Middle East, post-freedom violence erupted on a serious scale.

American military power was exerted in Vietnam in a disastrous manner, as the whole world now knows. But the policy of containment was not wholly without success. Large areas of the world have had a period of comparative tranquillity, undisturbed by foreign invasion or subversion on a serious scale, because of the American umbrella. Above all, a nuclear World War III has not broken out. The more extreme forms of repressive communism have not yet appeared in Africa, Asia or Latin America, and have become harder to maintain in Eastern Europe. For these favourable developments, the changes in policy made by the Russian leaders in the decade from 1953 must also receive some credit.

Nevertheless, the 1960s decade has shown dangerous tendencies not only in international relations, but in the structure of Western industrialized society, supposed to be one model for the newly developing countries (the other being communism). Both models have their respective advantages and drawbacks. A new cross current has appeared in history: the revolt of youth. In the Western society the new protest movement attacks not the abuses and deficiencies of the society, but its very root, its reliance upon a theory of liberalism. This has been the disturbing character-

16

istic of so many of the so-called protest movements. On the other side of what was once an iron curtain, the students and intellectuals are demanding more freedom to express themselves; they want freedom of speech, habeas corpus and all the appurtenances of liberalism. They too, are therefore challenging the roots of their society.

It is to be feared that if a world parliament of youth could be assembled it would rapidly come to blows. The Young Russians, Rumanians, and Czechs, while ardent in their loyalty to socialism, would be advocating tolerance, while the Young French, German, American and British students and intellectuals would be denouncing tolerance as a fraud, while at the same time expecting to be tolerated.

The point is that both establishments have run out of moral capital. The fact that most of their young critics are incoherent, illogical and ill-informed must not mislead anyone into thinking that they have no grounds or basis for their impatience. The cold war has ended not with a bang, nor a whisper, but with a hysterical yell. The real question is what went wrong?

The first thing that went wrong was the failure of the intellectual world to keep pace with the demands that society, stumbling its way through the consequences of a succession of technological revolutions, placed upon it. If one reads the books that have been produced in the last fifteen years on the structure of society, one finds endless sterile categorization, repetition of irrelevant ideas, sheer ignorance of history or even of current events, and trivial dogmatism; all this has given sociology a deservedly bad name.

The second has been the failure to keep a clear social objective before the public, particularly the ideal and purpose of greater equality of wealth and opportunity. The concept of the brotherhood of man, common to humanists and many religions, has simply got lost in the insane struggle for power of rival groups.

Equality as an Objective
Some writers have asserted without proof (or indeed evidence) that the achievement of equality is a moral objective which is

B   17 spreading continuously.[1] They believe that the desire for equality is continuously growing, and coming to include more attributes. The grounds for inequality, whichever they happen to be in a particular instance, are liable to be challenged, or disputed.

It is the purpose of this book to discuss the definition of equality, and the status of the concept. The achievement of equality, in some sense or other of that term, is undoubtedly an objective of policy. Evidence can be adduced to show that this is so.

Within national boundaries, tax systems exist. There is plenty of evidence that in most industrialized countries the basis of the system of direct taxation is a progressive principle. This means of course that the incomes of the individuals in each such country are taxed more than proportionately to their excess of income over some selected minimal income up to which no tax is imposed. The acceptance of this progressive principle means that each country has to that extent accepted the principle of trying to equalize the returns to individuals. Similarly of the economic relationships between nations, it can be said that relative poverty is acknowledged as a basis for gifts or for loans on special terms; whatever the political motives behind these decisions, it clearly has been decided (and this represents a consensus of opinion among the nations participating in international decisions) that the richer nations should make gifts to the poorer.

Whatever the theories behind these phenomena, it can be said that objectively the Western nations accept the duty of promoting equality both internally and internationally. Their actions betray them.

The Managerial World

At the same time that, for the first time in history, the world was rich enough to begin to remedy social injustices on a large scale without loss of efficiency, a new industrial revolution was taking place. The coming of age of electronic computers,

[1] See, for example, David Apter, *The Politics of Modernization* (London: Univ. Chicago Press, 1966), p. 73.

automation in factories and easier communication and transport has meant a total change in attitudes about management. The modern manager has immensely powerful weapons at hand, in the form of new communication techniques. The result of these techniques, combined with other factors, such as the importance of access to finance whether borrowed or internally generated by the firm, and the need for large-scale production and for the integration of economic activity, has been the coming of 'Big Business' on a scale hardly dreamed of by its critics in the 1880s or even the 1950s.

This is not the stage of analysis or description at which it would be appropriate either to approve or to deplore this change in the situation; all that is being done here is to note that it has happened. Professor Gardiner C. Means has done much to document and comment on this change as it has taken place over a thirty-year period. In his study of the early 1960s,[1] he observed how utterly different the managerial system, and the industrial system, were from the models of the neo-classical economists. The classical theory said, in effect, that market mechanisms would adjust prices so that manpower and capital would be directed to the most effective uses, and that the same market mechanism would adjust rewards to the factors of production so that they would receive a reward proportionate to their contribution to the end-result. These propositions were true of a world of small enterprises. They were quite irrelevant to a world dominated by the colossal corporations of 1960. They were just as inapplicable as the other classical theory, that full employment could be automatically achieved through adjustments in factor prices, with its corollary that if anyone was out of work, he was so deliberately and wilfully.

It may well be, as Gardiner Means suggests, that the 'administered' prices of the big monopolists and large-scale operators of today result in profits that are greater than the public interest allows. They are not competitive profits—the profits that would accrue under a genuinely competitive regime—nor are they

---

[1] *The Corporate Revolution in America* (Crowell-Collier, 1962).

profits determined by public policy. Big business, if it secures such returns, will have to face political pressures designed to help the community interest.

But the pressures, even if they shift the distribution of rewards into a slightly more equal direction, are not likely, short of an overthrow of the industrial system, to change completely the trend of events. The dilemma of politicians in this matter is illustrated by the ineffective struggle of some Europeans to resist the influx of American capital into Europe in the 1960s.[1] The $10 billions or so invested by American firms in Europe between 1958 and 1968 was attracted into key sectors of the European economy, especially into those which were advancing fast technologically and which had the highest potential for growth. Much of this investment was in fact financed from European sources, by subsidies from governments or by loans raised in Europe. National governments, alarmed at this trend, sometimes tried to halt the flow, or restrict it by imposing conditions. The most nationalistic of all governments, the French, oscillated between a policy of asking and encouraging the Americans to prefer France to the other Common Market countries and one of restriction, which promptly drove new American enterprise elsewhere. The fact that a single country, though normally a member of an integrated market, should approach this problem in a national context was significant.

American enterprise had several advantages in its development of the new economic frontier, Europe: first, that it was the off-shoot of easily the most powerful and successful economy in the world; secondly that it was supported at home in several key sectors by substantial government contracts to cover research and development expenses; and thirdly that, in relation to Europe, it could look at the market as a whole and not through French, German, British or any other local spectacles. Americans more than others were in this sense really good Europeans.

Moreover, even the Six, thanks to the exclusive policy imposed

[1] See *The American Challenge* by J-J. Servan-Schreiber (London: Hamish Hamilton, 1968).

on them by the French, could not as a whole risk too much hostility to American enterprise, which had the alternative of investing in Scandinavia, Spain or Great Britain.

It seems fairly clear that throughout the world big business is getting bigger, and, since American big business is predominant, this effectively means the spread of American economic power and influence. The governments of the world have in the last two decades, on the other hand, been getting smaller and smaller. There are now 140 or so independent states in the United Nations, and, as the foible of self-determination is pushed further and further, the number will undoubtedly grow, even though already taken to absurd length. The trouble in this sphere is that as the need for economic remedial action by the state gets even greater, in order to offset the misery and blight that the ruthless and impersonal search for profits and 'efficiency' imposes on society, so the burden of taxation and of government controls gets heavier. To attain some kind of equality, to provide minimum incomes for the sick, aged, disabled and unemployed, to give education and maintain other social services, modern states need to impose high taxation. A splinter state, of the size of San Marino or Monte Carlo (these have historical justification, but new enclaves can invent a tradition), has every chance of offering better tax and living conditions by living in the shadow of a friendly metropolitan power, allegiance to which they limit or reject outright. Countries the size of the Isles of Man or Wight, or Jersey or Guernsey, need little defence expenditure of their own, or can raise money from tourists and by neglect of social services.

While the craze for independence of small states persists, the great international companies inevitably become more powerful. They will have little to fear from parliaments of the calibre that the tiny new nations can elect. The trend towards ever smaller units of self-government will one day have to be reversed, since countervailing power will have to be mobilized against the great world monopolies which, to do them justice, have no ambitions to govern, and which are incapable of true political organization. The Common Market itself, as originally planned when the Treaty of Rome was signed, was clearly intended to be a first step towards a supranational political organ for economic planning and control. The control of monopolies was specifically mentioned in the Treaty.

Revolt of the Young

So much has been written on the classic pseudo-revolutionary year of 1968 that further comment might seem not to be needed. The reason for attempting once again to place the current unrest into perspective is that it is absolutely essential to identify what kinds of inequality are giving rise to the various frustrations in society.

The young, or relatively young, who have been most vocal are necessarily the most frustrated, not necessarily those afflicted by the gravest injustice or inequalities. However, to their credit from one point of view, by the violence and even by the extravagance of some of their protests, they have released the inhibitions of those whom decency, fear or sloth previously kept silent, and in Britain, for example, we know that a large proportion of the working-class are as racist as the Hitler Youth of not so long ago. Injustice is seen in many colours.

The original protests were anti-war and anti-racist, and their most vigorous expressions came in the United States. This followed on a long incubation period, beginning perhaps with the anti-nuclear bomb movement in Great Britain, or, further back than that, with the nationalist movement in India.

There can surely be no doubt that the Vietnam war was the final catalyst. It is again to the great credit of the generation of students that initiated rebellion and revolt, that they repudiated the official doctrine of violence that perpetuated escalation of a war against an impoverished people, and they repudiated too the doctrine of racial discrimination. These two principles were embodied in the reactions of students in America to the ideology of the existing establishment. That students should seek to be involved, as against their predecessors of the 1950s, who sought

22

a kind of disengagement from all involvement, in reaction to the sordid vulgarities of the McCarthy era, was a step forward.

Unfortunately, there was much else in society with which to become discontented, and there was enormous ignorance, and an almost complete absence of experience of responsibility among the protesters. Almost every group felt entitled to protest, if possible with some violence, against almost everything. There were sit-down strikes on ferries that were late starting; lecturers were physically prevented from lecturing, even on neutral topics; first-year students claimed the right to oversee the syllabus which they as yet had been unable to study.

The establishment was vulnerable. Ferries did not always run on time; lectures were often boring or irrelevant; syllabuses were mostly overdue for reform. But violence and ignorance could hardly remedy these deficiencies, nor could a new dogmatism usefully replace an old. What the young have done well, though they would repudiate it passionately, is reopen the channels of significant liberal debate.

The way that they see the situation is no doubt in many cases quite different. They adopted a set of teachers who were either wildly irrelevant, such as Debray or Che Guevara or Mao, or madly dilettante and irresponsible, as were so many popular sociologists. Some intellectuals of 1968 produced works that became drawing-room jokes, perhaps no more intended seriously than Nabokov's *Lolita* was intended to be a recipe for happy marital relations. As for the revolutionists, the machine-gun (i.e. weapon) in one's hand as a guarantee of sincerity and true revolutionary fervour, is a doctrine that Europe grew out of in the seventeenth century or earlier. It may make sense under a dictatorship and where villagers are truly oppressed, but not in the urban and suburban society of Western Europe, or the United States. Whatever else they need, it is not more assassination and more mindless violence. The tragic deaths of Robert Kennedy and Martin Luther King temporarily halted this poisonous mysticism.

The fact remains that authority was challenged successfully by students in 1968, in America, France, and Britain, and vigorously, if less successfully in West Germany and Yugoslavia. A world movement of youthful protest can be said to exist, dependent not upon a common programme or common cause, but resulting surely from common factors of the modern situation.

That situation was one of inadequate opportunity, and of dissatisfaction with the way that the world was being run. It is the task of this study to consider one set of factors in the general situation, those relating to economic equality, and to economic opportunity. It is not suggested that these are the only factors at work, but it is considered to be likely that the economic factors are important in the total situation.

Authority and Mass Media

A feature of the student revolt which marked off the 1960s quite distinctly from the 1950s was the challenge to authority, not to particular acts or policies. The very basis of authority was brought into question. For the first time since World War II, the capitalist world experienced what the communist world had for so long feared, an intellectual revolt that had to be considered, because it indeed was a questioning of the regime, not merely of its policies. A factor in this has been the growth of television.

This came of age in several different ways. First, has been its effect on popular education and on the popular imagination. As Buckminster Fuller said,[1] the new generation, post-1950, born into the television era, has absorbed knowledge about the pace of scientific and technological advance, even if they have not been educated in science. The whole youthful world knows now that much is possible. Science fiction has become one of the most popular forms of daydream, well embodied on the small screen. No one is any longer content with the argument that improvements in living are not feasible.

Secondly, television has brought home to audiences (ever since 1965) all over the world a mental picture of what modern

[1] Television interview on the BBC, July 1968.

war is like. This was one of the main reasons for the different impact of the Korean war and the Vietnam war upon the consciousness of the American, European and Australian peoples, to name only a few, and on other nations as well. Whether or not television documentaries and news coverage gave in 1968 a 'fair' picture of the war is a matter of dispute which can probably never be resolved. The point is that the picture was immediate, horrifying and productive of results. Among other things, it refuted again and again official claims as to the conduct and meaning of the war. Thus television, the most powerful propaganda medium that the world had ever known, worked to undermine authority.

Thirdly, television brought instant and aggressive criticism to bear, in England and to a lesser extent in the United States, upon the daily decisions of government. The result was that each successive government, after a brief period of instant popularity, founded largely upon some successful propaganda launched mainly on television itself, inevitably faced a later reaction in which everything that it did was held up to ridicule, or at least to severe questioning. A race of critics grew up, skilled in the art of unfair cross-examination of politicians. They became spokesmen of an opposition which would never itself have to meet the challenge of power, and which gradually revealed itself as an opposition not to policies but to all government.

In the United States, Madison Avenue was called in to increase the popularity rating of politicians among a fairly ignorant public. The same technique was borrowed in England. In America the weapon turned against those who used it. First, as the claims of advertisers and hucksters were gradually seen to be self-interested and false, so claims on behalf of politicians and governments couched in similar terms seemed to fall into the same category. The reaction was so severe that no statement of fact by politician, and no claim, was considered to be true.

Secondly, once the politicians resorted to advertising techniques, and began themselves to take Gallup-style polling seriously, they became victims to the rapid tides of public opinion. They lost their position as statesmen, too lofty to be guided by other than a few immutable general principles.

The instant challenge to every act, and indeed to every word, of a politician was moreover a threat that no human being could meet, and when all is said and done politicians are but human.

A situation of very great danger to representative government has thus been worsened. The surviving regimes include those which ruthlessly suppress opposition to their views, especially on television. The Australian Government is far less liberal to the ABC than the British Government is to the BBC, and is for that reason (among others) much firmer in the saddle. The de Gaulle government in 1968 pushed its partisan control of broadcasting to notorious lengths, exciting intense minority opposition but gaining massive majority support, at least in the short run, for electoral purposes.

The effects of the mass media are the subject of many surveys, but no attempt will be made to summarize their results. Three broad changes are, however, very noticeable and may be hypothetically identified. First, public opinion—a much derided but meaningful term—seems to have become noticeably more volatile. Politicians have always been liable to rise or fall in public esteem in very short periods; an unfortunate phrase used by a prime minister on Friday may reduce his popularity significantly by the following Tuesday. This kind of thing has, it appears, been very much enhanced. The violent swings of view apply to other matters than the personal popularity of individual politicians—to particular wars or riots, for example. The reaction against participation by America in the Vietnam war was far more violent and emotional than against participation in the Korean war, for a number of reasons, one of which was undoubtedly the much greater coverage of horrific incidents that American television screens portrayed on the latter occasion.

Secondly, the mass media have reduced the credibility of all official statements. This was partly an objective result, as it were, of picking up military leaders' bromides and showing them up, but it was also due to the weakness of commercial television. The millions of dollars and pounds spent on advertising have, in my view, at least begun to show a truly counter-productive pay-off. If a system claims daily and nightly that a series of products are what they are not,[1] a point is reached when no statement is believed. For many recipients, an automatic negative effect occurs, or the statement is blotted out altogether. This is a hypothesis that needs testing to establish its quantitative value at any time, but that it has operated to some extent is established by direct observation; one thing the younger generation displayed in 1967 which they did not display in 1957 was considerable disillusion with advertising, main prop of free enterprise marketing, and this disillusion went deeper than an objection to huckstering.

Thirdly, and much more positively, the mass media have made the whole game of transmitting information and social criticism much more fun. It is true that the immense effectiveness of the propaganda media has put power into irresponsible, and sometimes unscrupulous, hands, except in those countries where a government monopoly has ensured that it stays under more responsible, but often more unscrupulous, control.

Equality as a Goal
With so many discontents, and so many unresolved questions of government to be answered, it may seem strange to keep returning to the central topic of equality as an objective, or goal, of policy. The point is that, as advanced in more detail below, equality, or some movement towards greater equality, is to a large extent still an acceptable goal. If it can be achieved, society itself will be modified in consequence of the economic change. More equal societies produce different leaders, and create a different atmosphere or framework for not only economic but general social policy. The challenge to the excesses of authority is more likely to be soundly based and effective in an equal society

[1] Not all advertisers follow this policy; some of the most successful are scrupulously 'factual'.

than in one with gross inequalities, where protest tends to become hysterical and violently extremist.

This is of course a liberal hope, and one which many revolutionaries would repudiate. However, the alternatives seem both more dangerous and less likely to be realized. Can one imagine a succession of tyrannies in the developed countries, each vying with its predecessor for brutality and suppression? Whether originating from the right or the left such dictatorships would fail to please the politically-minded centre of modern society, or the non-politically-minded middle class. Greater equality is not perhaps a sufficient objective, but, it may be submitted, it is a necessary one as a first step to a reform of government.

CHAPTER 2

MINIMUM PRACTICABLE INEQUALITY

The Principle

Equality is easy to define and measure; it occurs when every income receiver gets the same sum in income. But inequality may take innumerable forms, and by any standard of measuring it must be arbitrary. No one seriously advocates, as an ideal, perfect equality of incomes, first because such extreme equality would be unenforceable under any known system of government, and secondly, because it is believed that persons with skills would not use their abilities fully enough unless there were differences between the pay packets of skilled and unskilled workers. Thirdly, as Mr Douglas Jay pointed out at the beginning of the 1960s,[1] the great majority of mankind, including most socialists, probably believe that the more skilful and more diligent workers *deserve* some extra reward.

The principle then is not to set a target of perfect equality, but rather to aim at something that can be called 'minimum practicable inequality'. Mr Jay defined this as the amount which would ensure that workers' talents were exercised so that society might benefit to the full from their employment. In times of scarcity of certain skills, this 'minimum inequality' might result in payments far below that which market forces, left to themselves, would dictate. The market tends to produce quasi-rents, as Marshall called them, surpluses of payment to scarce factors over and above that minimum which would be necessary to call human capacities fully into production. These quasi-rents disappear only when the supply of skilled labour has been adequately increased

Mr Jay's approach is an ethical or moral one. In his view,

[1] In *Socialism in the New Society*, Faber, 1962.

income receivers do not *deserve* to receive more than that minimum which will ensure that they contribute their skill fully to production, yet they do deserve to receive some difference graded to their skill, but below the full market assessment of it. In an earlier book[1] Jay had deprecated very heavy taxation of earned incomes, on the grounds, first, that large earned incomes did not then add up to a significant proportion of total national income, and, secondly, because the very high salaries that some people received were 'usually' paid in return for services that, on a broad view, were highly important to the community, and thirdly, such incomes were often necessarily saved for the greater part, rather than consumed.

Aristotle had anticipated Douglas Jay. He thought that societies should set limits to the degree of economic inequality associated with a hierarchical system, on the grounds that otherwise envy, and hence political instability, would ensue, and give rise to civil conflict. He too therefore implied a principle of minimum practicable inequality, an inequality sufficient to keep the needed hierarchical system working but not so great as to give rise to revolution.

Sociologists, and economists influenced by sociologists, nowadays seem to be inclined to agree with Aristotle. They see little prospect that society can be run without some form of hierarchical ranking and order. They often quote in support of this position some modified version of Pareto's law. Pareto is said to have found empirically a remarkable constancy in the shape of the cumulative curve describing income level against numbers of incomes in different societies. The form of the curve did not vary much in space, in time or with social organization, according to Stigler. The deduction to be made from this was that inequality could not be significantly modified unless the whole structure of society was changed. The nature of men, or their class relationships, or something fundamental, had to be altered, before any major change in income distribution could be introduced.

[1] *The Socialist Case* (London: Faber, 1947).

Steps towards minimum economic inequality (in earned income) do not in fact have to wait quite so ominously as this may sound. By a consensus, progressive taxation has been adopted and maintained, and other economic changes favouring equality have come about. These include shifts in the distribution of manpower, and a narrowing of the dispersion of incomes in advanced industrial communities, if not over the whole range at least over a wide range of activities.

The principle of minimum necessary inequality may then be defended as embodying a consensus view in many societies, and one which is partly attainable and wholly rational. The general proposition is, as Professor Tumin has implied,[1] that if the personnel necessary for tasks that are fundamentally important to society are scarce, and if to induce some personnel to do these tasks various kinds of unequal rewards have to be paid, then it is rational for the society to pay such awards to obtain a correct manpower allocation. It is important to note that the principle is conditional. To the extent that other motives prevail, the system of differential rewards may in part be unnecessary or even harmful.

Unearned Incomes

The principle of minimum necessary inequality has so far been discussed in relation to (by implication) an abstract model of a world in which all incomes are earned in respect of current services rendered. In the real world many incomes are inherited, or the result of investment. Many possibilities then arise. The mechanisms whereby those who have earned wealth become still wealthier, and by which they possibly acquire power, and through power yet further wealth, may be very different from the mechanisms that led to the original differentiation between rewards for work done.

Douglas Jay, in 1947, argued that the central aim of socialists should be the abolition of all inherited incomes. He thought that there was no abuse in a man who saved and invested in a govern-

[1] See 'On Equality', *American Sociological Review*, 1963.

ment stock, but a very great abuse if a man owned a 'vast' country mansion, and a 'park of a thousand acres', or if he lived on the income from a large block of slum property if these assets were inherited, and were to be passed on in due course to his children. In 1947 the capital gains of ordinary stock were not easy to foresee, and that form of investment was not directly criticized. While inherited assets as such may be reasonable targets of taxation, it is not quite obvious why particular kinds of property should be liable to heavier rates. In the particular historical situation of 1947 there may have been some lingering relics of an ancient landlordism that needed to be stamped out. Even if this be granted, however, it seems doubtful that differential rates of inheritance tax would have been the best way for the state to accomplish this purpose. Nor is there much doubt that Jay's list exhibits a particular bias with which not even all socialists agreed even in 1947.

But studies of economic growth have often shown that inequalities associated with a protected position for landed property owners, or landed élites, have had specially unfortunate consequences because they have been associated with stagnation in the economy. In a recent study[1] of the association of major groups of factors (social and economic) with growth, the point was made that the break-up of the landed élites' control of the agricultural surplus in a country was a precondition for the take-off stage in economic development, so perhaps Jay's prejudices have wider application than internal evidence suggested.

As things have turned out, those who invested in land in Great Britain, particularly in urban land, but also in rural, have done best of all in increasing the value of their assets since 1947, while investors in ordinary stocks have fared, on average, nearly as well, and the holders of government or other fixed-interest securities have suffered relatively worst. Inheritance taxes have

[1] Irma Adelman and Cynthia Taft Morris, 'A Factor Analysis of the Interrelationships between Social, Political Variables and *per capita* Gross National Product', *Quarterly Journal of Economics*, 1965.

mitigated, but by no means removed, inequalities due to inheritance, partly because ingenious lawyers and accountants have progressively discovered legal methods of avoiding the full payment of duties on the original assets held. Wealthy people have passed on wealth to their heirs through special devices like trusts or skilfully arranged gifts.

However it is to be administered, the tax principle should clearly be different for capital than it is for income. Capital holdings have the possibility of growth. A capital gains tax, such as has operated in Britain in recent years, provides some offset to the tendency for the dispersion of wealth to become more unequal.

The alarming point about wealth inequality as compared with earned income inequality is that it tends to be worse, not better, the more affluent the society. Successful attempts seem to have been made during short, intensive periods of reform to reduce the inequality, due, in industrialized countries, to the uneven distribution of property. Such periods in Britain were that of the Lloyd George budgets between 1906 and 1912, and the period of World War II and its aftermath, down to 1951. Between 1938 and 1950 property incomes fell from some 22 per cent of gross domestic product to some 12 per cent, according to Dudley Seers' calculations, but this trend seems to have been reversed between 1951 and 1961, when inequality of wealth increased in consequence largely of a continuing inflation.

If the full effects of inflation had been foreseen, it is surely arguable that more might have been done to offset its extremely regressive effects.

Although the evidence is imperfect, the general position in regard to income and wealth distribution in Great Britain is clear. There was a tendency towards greater equality of post-tax incomes and wealth between 1938 and 1957. Employee income, together with social insurance payments, were rising faster over that period than other incomes,[1] as a result of full employment

[1] See quotations in M. Lipton, *Assessing Economic Performance* (London: Staples, 1968).

C

from about 1941 onwards, and the strengthened bargaining position of labour after World War II, with the consequent elimination of a large sector of the working population on the dole or in underpaid jobs.

As an illustration it may be pointed out that the top 1 per cent of earners received only about half as big a share (8 per cent against 16 per cent) of total incomes in 1960 as they did in 1938. Similarly the percentage of total capital belonging to the top 1 per cent of owners was drastically reduced, to 42 per cent from some 56 per cent.

Many would agree that it is not easy to be happy even about the existing distribution of wealth and income. Wealth is still much more unequally distributed in a country like Great Britain than income, yet inequality of income has at least *some* rational thinking behind it, since earned income reflects an individual's current or recent efforts, however imperfectly. The Chicago school of economists, while opposing severe tax rates on incomes, on the grounds that incomes must be allowed to perform their allocative function freely, urge quite consistently that inheritance taxes should be severe.

Rewards for Managers

The managerial revolution, as a conscious idea, has been accepted for at least thirty years, but its precise implications are still being worked out, and certainly are not supported by 'consensus' opinion.

One penetrating analyser[1] of the managerial set-up has strongly argued that a reward system for managers is needed to meet the 'functional and social needs' of a very special class of persons, namely those who provide the skills needed in a large-scale organization. This in turn is necessary for modern forms of economic activity to be possible. If we accept Mr Marris' line of argument, we should have to agree that large rewards for managers were appropriate.

[1] Robin Marris, in *The Economic Theory of 'Managerial' Capitalism* (London: Macmillan, 1964).

Marris points out that widespread use of a committee system does not cut out the need for a hierarchical chain of command. A committee system works well when it is backed up by an efficient hierarchy.

A hierarchy implies a pyramid for the organizational chart, and if a pyramid is inevitable for the chain of command, it is difficult not to accept a corresponding salary structure. This is particularly so in any society in which income and status are closely associated, as it is in most 'Western-style' economies. It becomes difficult to arrange, or even visualize a system in which the money paid in income goes down, while the prestige and standing of the recipient goes up. Salaries become status symbols in the organizational world. They are wanted as much as badges of success as for the additional comforts that they bring. There is nowadays, furthermore, some international trade in skilled managers, so it would be difficult for a Chancellor of the Exchequer to interfere both directly and drastically.

Can the principle of minimum necessary inequality be stretched so far as to include the need for differential managerial salaries? What is really involved in the hierarchical case?

The claim that, for the managerial class, at least, a pyramidal system is 'inevitable' seems to rest on three foundations, first, that it can hardly be avoided in any industrial society, since managers are in a position to affect, if not to determine the levels of their own rewards; secondly, on the need to provide both an incentive and an adequate background within the existing society for the manager to function at whatever 'level' in the hierarchy he is to occupy; and thirdly, the idea that members of firms and society at large will view the levels of salaries as badges of status.

There is considerable force in this case, which cuts across ideological systems and seems to apply, *mutatis mutandis*, in a wide range of industrialized societies, whether communistic or capitalistic in name. Whole series of policies for the training of managerial manpower, and for its deployment, are being based on the hypothesis that the hierarchical argument is sound.

For example, efforts are being made in the 1960s to provide a training or an education for management on a huge scale in Europe, both West and East, in imitation of the success of the business schools in the United States. Many of these efforts are likely to produce candidates for management posts with a deeper formal training in modern management techniques than, on average, they would have attained before the new courses were set up.

The difficulty in accepting the theory of a 'necessary' hierarchy is that it is hard to define what is the 'minimum necessary' in the way of inequality in order to optimize the system.[1] Views of what is necessary seem bound in practice to be highly subjective. One symptom of how quickly such an argument results in doubtful claims, is the high starting salary claimed often with little justification by the products of the business schools. These claims probably are of minor social importance, since after some trial and error, market forces will take care of them,

[1] Sir Roy Harrod has suggested, in a review of Professor Lipton's book,* that it might not be prudent to push any argument for equality to an extreme, since no one really knows enough about 'high civilization and culture', to determine the social and economic value of élites. Harrod supposes that the progress of human welfare must in the long run depend upon 'high culture', and that this may, in some sense as yet unknown with any certainty, depend upon the existence of a minority of intellectuals. Above all, Harrod adds with a perceptive insight, perhaps the able men with good second-class intellects, who hold key positions, may need to mingle often with persons of 'pure alpha quality', who are the real salt of society, although some of them may not themselves be qualified to run affairs, or even to make their own living. This view of the élite may be interpreted as referring to groups of superlative back-room boys (and girls). If such people are needed by society a market system can support them, or some system of state salaries. But perhaps Harrod is hinting not at the need for boffins, so much as the need for a certain kind of society in which inequalities are tolerated, for the atmosphere of free inventiveness and criticism that they imply. The 'little circles' which Proust both derided and cherished, perhaps have an important leavening role to perform.

* *Economic Journal*, Sept. 1968, a review by Harrod of *Assessing Economic Performance* by M. Lipton (Staples Press, London: 1968).

and the actual salaries paid settle down, although of course an element of monopolistic success may accrue if young (trained) managers are scarce and there is a fashion for employing them.

The graver social changes would seem to be that some hard and fast new social barrier gets itself established, once the hierarchical pattern has been accepted for the manager, especially if at the same time it is rejected for all others. The industrial world then would allow a division to creep in between the managers and the managed. The inflexibility of any such social system might become very great. For a parallel in the past, one has only to look at the difficulties that occurred, in the later stages of the use of a distinction in the British civil service, between the administrative and all other classes.

If this danger is to be avoided, either the hierarchical principle must be dropped, and the case for any necessary differential payments put to some other basis, or it must be modified and perhaps extended. A generalized principle of inequality must be found. Some jobs must be deemed to be so necessary to society and so difficult to fill, or so honorific, that those who take them are entitled to more pay than the average worker in the average job.

When society faces acute economic difficulties, the decision-makers, including the government authorities, find themselves under pressure to untie, or at worst to cut, this Gordian knot. The exercise sometimes takes the form of striving to maintain a prices and incomes policy. Under this, an attempt is made to decide, in effect, what rates of pay are 'socially necessary' for what jobs at the particular historical and economic conjuncture at which the economy as a whole, and one individual industry in particular, may find themselves.

If the task of settling prices and income is left largely to market forces, some kind of equilibrium will be reached, but incomes are under strong pressure to rise too fast, from a social point of view, in times of inflation. If, on the other hand, governmental authorities through an arbitration system at which they

37

are officially represented, as well as the employees, or through a prices and incomes board, such as Britain has been operating for a few years—come directly on the scene, they are accepting a new major responsibility. This is one which they have partly to accept under almost any known system. But in a country where it is politically important that inequalities should be kept 'minimal' the determination of classes of wages and salaries in the end gets referred, whether they like it or not, at least to a series of advisory bodies, and sometimes to boards nominally given 'power' by statute to determine each issue. The trouble is that as the determinations take place piecemeal, each sector of wage or salary earners clamours for their individual increase, and may be prepared to create difficulties by so-called 'industrial action' if they are not satisfied. The alternative of a simultaneous determination of *all* salary and wage-earners' rewards hardly holds out any prospects of being any less contentious, and indeed for obvious reasons would be much more so, since some reasonably 'contented' industries might get aroused, while final settlement of all issues would in any case proceed at an uneven pace, so bringing back eventually the disputed individual issues.

Wages and Incomes Determination under different Systems
With an all too familiar conceit, British spokesmen are sometimes heard to claim that the new Prices and Incomes Board is breaking new ground, or setting an example to the world, by introducing a fresh element into the compulsory regulations of wages. In fact, there have been numerous attempts made in different countries over many years to evolve such a system. Central pay negotiation is, indeed, common practice in Scandinavia, the Netherlands and other European countries. The Netherlands began a pay policy in 1945 which was unique because of its combination of collective bargaining with statutory regulation and government intervention. The Netherlands became the only country in Europe where pay settlements could only be put into effect with government approval, and where maximum as well as minimum pay rates were established,

side by side with a direct and comprehensive system of price control.[1]

Control of prices was regarded in the Netherlands, as in Norway, as an essential adjunct to a wages policy. It was considered to be a practical way of indirectly controlling profits, and of containing one of the main economic changes likely to lead to claims for pay increases. Price control has also played a considerable role in Austria, Belgium, France, and in recent years in the United Kingdom. Under the comprehensive system in the Netherlands, producers of all goods and services had to notify any price increases to the Ministry of Economic Affairs with a justification. For some essential items, like bread, milk, margarine and fuel (the list was formerly longer), the Ministry must still be consulted in advance. The Ministry, if it concludes, after investigation, that some price rise is unjustified, tries to persuade the industry to modify the rise by voluntary agreement, but its request is backed up by the possibility of using compulsory powers.

Consumer subsidies for food are one means whereby the Norwegian Government can influence pay negotiations.

The Dutch system of pay control was originally not only comprehensive, but also somewhat rigid. It was found that, for instance, the standard system could not easily be applied to piece-workers[2] and in any case the system could be got round by 'over-grading' workers, so permitting higher rates of pay. Over the twenty post-war years, the influence of the government on incomes has indeed been steadily diminishing, and there has been a deliberate effort made to allow greater differentiation in pay increases between different branches of the Ministry, and for different occupations.

Thus, in 1956, a *maximum* increase of 6 per cent was permitted centrally and it was left to the branches to distribute this increase.

[1] For the points covered here see 'Incomes in Post-war Europe' Part 2 of the *Economic Survey of Europe in 1965* (Geneva: E.C.E., 1967).

[2] The proportion of piece-workers rose from 45 to 64 per cent between 1951 and 1954.

In 1959 the Government initiated a new system, approving (in advance) the decision of individual branches, provided that the branches could show increased productivity. This was quite a revolutionary new criterion in view of the so-called 'solidarity' principle which hitherto underlay the co-ordination of pay increases in Nordic countries, a principle which had been applied for some decades to iron out historically determined discrepancies in rewards.

Difficulties arose immediately the new productivity criterion was introduced. They arose partly because of the lack of basic information. No statistics on productivity existed for numbers of industries and, even where they did, problems of equity remained. Formulas for sorting out these difficulties became so complicated that government intervention was needed, and this in itself aroused criticism.

A fresh framework for policy was introduced in 1963. Official intervention was reduced, and specific criteria for pay adjustments were abandoned. But the new scheme came into force just at the time when labour was relatively scarce.

The result was a reversal of trend, and a demand from the unions for an end to all governmental controls over pay. The beautifully working system of a decade earlier began to succumb under the same kinds of intense pressure as have afflicted prices and incomes policies in so many countries. By 1966, with its back to the wall, so to speak, the Netherlands Government was trying to restrict permitted increases in wages to a ceiling of 7 per cent. The best available guess seemed in 1967 officially to be that past trends of increase (and relative shifts) in productivity and pay can be extrapolated at least down to 1970. Thus even the country with the strongest predilection for wages control has found this policy difficult to enforce.

In other northern European countries there were, up to the mid-1960s, no such elaborate productivity-geared incomes policies as the Netherlands had developed in the period 1959-63. Trade unions usually pressed for equal increases for all, subject to the qualification that 'solidarity' must prevail. Solidarity means that there should be equal pay for equal work,[1] that wage levels should not be varied because of differing commercial or other circumstances. It is a principle therefore that is related to the 'standard wage' concept. Enterprises that cannot pay the wage demanded should go out of business.

Long Period Equalization of Pay Rates[2]

Hierarchical structures persist in modern societies, but they are not necessarily rigid. Indeed, a reasonable hypothesis would be that a static hierarchical social system could not have survived in competition with modernized systems unless it had become adaptable. Sociological surveys have indicated that no modern complex society yet started could correctly be described as closed or static.[3] Class barriers in these societies exist but are not insurmountable. There is a substantial infiltration from lower to upper orders of society, as well as shifts in lateral and downward directions.

Nevertheless, long-term study of relative occupational distribution and pay structure suggests that, though by no means completely rigid, class stratification is set into fairly firm patterns which seem to have been strangely difficult to change in any fundamental way. At the very least, the stratification is firm and lasting enough to limit severely the competition for higher-paid jobs. As Adam Smith and other classical economists had foreseen, only a major expansion in education (publicly financed, as Adam Smith thought that it would have to be) could effect the supply of skilled workers. Since World War II the education system in Great Britain was deliberately adapted to serve this purpose, and Routh has calculated that between 1935 and 1955, higher professional pay fell from 395 to 269 per cent of the all-class average, and lower professional pay from 188 to 114 per cent. It is not unreasonable to associate this shift towards equality

[1] Wage differentials between occupations or trades are not tolerated unless they can be shown to be related to differences in work performed.

[2] See especially Guy Routh, *Occupation and Pay in Great Britain, 1906-60* (Cambridge: Univ. Press, 1965).

[3] See Bendix and Lipset.

with the substantial increases both in the proportion of the population who became full-time university students, and in the public grants made for study at universities and technical colleges.

But for wage-earners the net result of short periods when gaps were narrowed (despite others when they widened) was that over the long period from 1914 to 1960 skilled average wages rose by some 800 per cent and unskilled average wages by 850 per cent, as Routh points out. It seems that it has been quite extraordinarily difficult to gain anything more than a temporary improvement in the *relative* pay of any occupation, although there are exceptions for particular categories. One pay change leads to another, and is made the basis of a claim that relative values should be preserved. A striking feature of the national pay structure in Britain in the twentieth century seems to have been this comparative rigidity in relative pay rates.

Sometimes relative pay rates do get changed, and a different kind of rigidity operates. For example, groups of employees like policemen, civil servants and judges may find themselves relatively worse off after an upward shift in most industrial wages. But these groups do not necessarily respond as if in a purely 'economic' situation, in which wages as the price of labour bring supply and demand into equilibrium. The services are continued for quite a time without a fall-off in supply. After a while, however, the so-called 'ratchet' effect is likely to reassert itself. The policemen, civil servants, or other disfavoured groups will, by their temporary lag, have built up a strong grievance, and are likely to run a vigorous campaign to restore those differentials that seem appropriate to British society.

While only major changes in the structure of society itself, caused mainly by education, have helped to reduce some of the differentials by operating on the supply side of the labour market, even these have stopped far short of achievable equalization in Britain. An investigation by Professor Routh showed that among a group of draughtsmen, where father's occupation was studied, there was a considerable under-representation of the sons of semi-skilled and unskilled manual workers. Even allowing for the possibility that inherited abilities are not randomly distributed, the results suggest that talent that could be used is not being used, as a result of inequality of opportunity.

If Routh's analysis is correct, the conclusions that follow are, first, that minimum inequality has been far from attained in Britain in the twentieth century, even though, on other evidence, some greater overall equality has been gained; secondly, that to work through a prices or incomes policy alone would not be a very effective way of creating greater equality, owing to the rigidity of the pay structure and the ratchet effect; thirdly, that only the classic remedy effectively remains, to raise expenditure on education, so increasing the supply of suitable persons for the skilled occupations.

Unfortunately, this last prescription, which is not only time-honoured but pointing in a direction that is appealing for other reasons,[1] is open to question. How can anyone be sure that widening the entry to higher education will diminish inequality? The assumption on which such a conclusion is based must be that in this instance market forces will indeed operate effectively, precisely the point that was denied in the earlier part of the analysis. Will an increased number of graduates bring down the wages of graduates so as to offset some inequitable differential? Or will not the professions rather close their ranks, fight for their differentials successfully, and by exercising various forms of political power effectively relegate many of the new graduates to unemployment and subversion? In the context of some developing countries, this question is not merely rhetorical; it pinpoints a major social dilemma.

Elites and Social Stratification

If the ideal, acceptable by a consensus of opinion in many modern, or modernizing societies, is that of some kind of

---

[1] Education is of course an end as well as a means. There are reasons to believe that its effect as a means is often underrated. Both American and Japanese experience suggest that a widespread high level of general popular educational expenditure has unexpectedly high potential economic returns.

'minimum practicable inequality', the question still has to be raised 'minimal in relation to what goals?' The inequalities under discussion are economic, but what is practicable and what is minimal may be governed by non-economic factors.

Social scientists have often concluded, either from general reasoning or from observation, that any society whatsoever tends to exhibit some measure of social stratification, whether or not this is so rigid as to be described as hierarchical. Some social units within the society are ranked as inferior or superior to others in a scale of social worth, and in many social systems the rewards available in the society, some of them classifiable as economic, are distributed unequally on the grounds of this inferiority or superiority. It is hard to envisage any but the most primitive and also small-scale society in which stratification did not occur.

Stratification may be based on roles or attributes. A man may play a different role from a child or a woman, or in a family group the father may have a distinct role. Ranking may be based on intrinsic or acquired characteristics, or on leadership gained from outstanding conformity or nonconformity, or on property differentials. The possible variety of arrangements is presumably very large in principle, and observation confirms that a wide variety of bases for ranking has been used. Whatever the basis, some kind of social stratification seems to be so common as to be acceptable as universal.[1]

Social stratification as such, though not any particular version of it, may be justified in relation to an economic goal, if it is a necessary condition for an economically viable society. This at once means, however, that there must be limits other than economic to practicable economic equality. Because the required minimum of social differentiation between individuals or classes usually is closely linked with differentiated economic rewards.

[1] This is a modified interpretation of the definitions stated by Professor Melish Tumin in 'On Equality', an important essay in the *American Sociological Review*, 1963.

The point has to be made, because the classic line of liberal thinking tended to stress the concept of the individual and his rights, regardless of the issues raised by his social relationships. To recapitulate briefly two and a half centuries of theory is dangerous, but to sharpen the issue a single statement may suffice.

Modern egalitarianism started with Rousseau, Jefferson and Bentham, who of course were fully aware that there were different mental and physical endowments among men, and that in this sense there were inequalities.[1] When they asserted that each 'man' (human being in some contexts) should be treated as equal, they were making a big claim for the rights of the individual as such. Each individual human being is to be relatively equal to each other human being in respect of the law, for example, or of some other functioning of society.

As Professor Hart puts it, justice is traditionally thought of as involving the principle 'treat like cases alike', and he points out that this principle is incomplete and cannot be consistently applied unless we define in what respects any set of human beings has to resemble each other to be treated as 'alike'.

The egalitarians, faced by issues of this kind, fall back on the notion that the channels should be improved for the passage of one individual from one social group to another. John Stuart Mill deplored the strongly marked demarcations that separated the different skilled trades of that craftsmen's era that preceded, and at the same time undermined, the early stages of the industrial revolution. Mill thought that the distinctions went too far and amounted almost to 'an hereditary distinction of caste'. So, like Adam Smith before him, he looked to a massive dose of education to smooth the transitions, to make more alike those who were unlike, and to enable society to usher in that perfect equality of opportunity for every man that was so desirable. This trend of thinking has lasted down to the present day, and the doctrine of

[1] Nevertheless, to this day, anti-egalitarians triumphantly point out that physically and mentally men are not all equal, as though this had been overlooked.

45

equality of opportunity is to be found in all current programmes of egalitarians.

Equality of opportunity seems undoubtedly to be 'obviously' in accordance with natural justice, especially to those brought up in a social system with gross biases towards privileged education, and inequalities in opportunity. That there is much to be said on both moral and on practical grounds for giving greater opportunities to groups that have special difficulties in getting educated may be substantiated from many sources.[1] Some of these very sound arguments and statistics will be used in discussing the social and economic reforms that the modernizing countries need.

But there are two points of principle that must be carefully considered. First, is the doctrine of equality of opportunity to be pushed to the point that all existing social arrangements are abandoned? Some would say yes, and others violently oppose such propositions. Is there any consensus on this issue? It will be argued that there is. Secondly, what are the opportunities to which the equality of opportunity policy leads? Do they not presuppose the continuation of just that kind of élite which the egalitarian policy was intended to eliminate?

This second question is one with practical implications that have already become issues of public debate, both in developing and in industrialized countries. Far from equalizing society as a whole, the great expansion of tertiary education in the last twenty years in countries so different as India, Thailand and Great Britain has created a new 'meritocracy' with claims to higher economic rewards, and often to differentiation from the social levels of its parents. This has created social tensions owing to the scepticism of the public that has not had any contact with tertiary education other than being taxed to pay for it, and to the self-confidence of the tertiary-educated who know that they are in scarce supply. As even tertiary education, expensive as it is, is not a complete education, further training is required in most

[1] Particularly from evidence collected by committees of enquiry into educational systems.

cases, and the demand for high differential rewards after long apprenticeships tends to become ever more insistent.

As for the first question, its most eloquent exponent has perhaps been Professor George Morgan.[1] He denounces modern equalitarianism[2] for its 'temporal atomism', by which he means its implication that each individual should begin life 'all over again', from scratch as it were, like Adam or Robinson Crusoe. In his view, because of this implication, to apply the principle of equal opportunity involves the abolition of the family. Each individual is supposed, under that principle, to work his way up from an equal start towards his own distinctive achievement, but he is, if the principle is rigidly applied, not to be allowed to pass on any of his gains, spiritual or material, to his offspring. Once he is gone, the whole process begins again so that each new generation has to be hatched out, as it were, in a standardized beginning process, and reared in a homogenized social matrix, not a specific human family. But, in Morgan's view, the family is the 'historical microcosm', the organized unit through which the great traditions of human civilization are maintained. That which is transmitted through the family is a spiritual as well as a material wealth, and to cut this thread of communication on the grounds that some children thereby gain an 'unfair' advantage is to create a series of 'broken segments' called individual lives. It is presumptuous to maintain that to attain greater equality at the cost of abolishing the basic civilizing unit of society necessarily represents a moral gain.

The argument still applies even if material wealth is separated from spiritual. All economic wealth could revert to the state treasury at the death of the individual. There would still remain the question of how to enforce equality of opportunity, and

[1] In his article 'Human Equality', which appeared in *Ethics*, 1943.

[2] Modern writers, especially in America, seem to prefer this to the older form 'egalitarianism'. Possibly equalitarianism is less pedantic and thus more egalitarian, than egalitarianism, but since the word 'equalitarian' is offensive and 'egalitarian' necessary, the older form has some merit; the two words are used to mean the same and chosen in relation to the context.

some egalitarians would indeed maintain that social and other advantages should not be allowed to accrue to children of relatively well-off parents.

A consensus view of this issue would probably be neither so extreme as Morgan's in its scepticism of some measure of greater equality of opportunity for all, nor as that of the egalitarians, who would indeed wish to abolish all 'privilege', including whatever might accrue from growing up within a well-educated and successful family. A middle view, that has some basis, would be that the family should not be forcibly abolished. Inheritance taxes should be varied effectively, so as to reduce economic inequalities arising from legacies. Publicly financed schooling should be so much improved that private schooling was left to eccentric or special groups of parents and guardians, but no official attempt would be made to suppress a private school system altogether.

Whether this, or some variant of it, is the best solution to the problem, anyone who advocates, as the liberal egalitarians so frequently advocate, equality of opportunity as the main method of reform, must face this difficulty. Equality of opportunity if pushed far enough would demand a total change in society, and some of these changes would cause social costs of great magnitude. How far the abolition of the family should be regarded as a cost is a matter for discussion, and for reaching an agreed valuation.

The conclusion to each of these discussions seems always to be the same. Equality of income and wealth is a reasonable objective of policy, but it should not be sought regardless of social costs. Its value is relative, and not absolute. Nevertheless there are whole areas of the world which seem ripe for major changes in income and wealth distribution. In practice, the danger seems more often to be that the public authorities will fail to go far enough, not that they may go too far.

CHAPTER 3

EDUCATION AND INEQUALITY

If education is to be the principal means for reducing inequality in a society, two decisions have to be taken. The first question is how much, or what proportion of the national income, should be spent in total on education, and the second is how best should a given expenditure be distributed, to attain the objective. In practice, the reduction of existing inequality is not usually, or indeed ever, the sole objective of educational expenditure, so these questions are never resolved solely in relation to that purpose. But reducing or, at the very least, restraining the growth of inequality is usually one of the objects of educational policy. In that context, how can these questions be answered?

Education takes many forms. There is education in the home, not only for infants but for older children; there are many forms of social education, and there is the impact of the mass media, films, television programmes, books, magazines and periodicals. There are both religious education and secular education in private schools. Public direct expenditure on education is only the topping-off item, the one that is intended to make certain that a minimum standard is reached by all.

Public expenditure, intended to secure this minimum standard, may be very heavy, and a great burden on the national income as standards are raised. Even so, it does not necessarily comprise the heaviest outgoing that the nation is making, in any period, on education. This honour belongs to 'incomes foregone'—the sacrifice of earnings that pupils make by neglecting to earn in order to learn, once they are old enough to be permitted to be employed.

It used to be thought, not so many decades ago, that England and Wales could not afford to send children to school at twelve and thirteen years of age, precisely because the output of these

D

children could not be lost without bankruptcy facing the country. When the school-leaving age was raised to fifteen, there were doubts expressed as to how commercial houses could remain viable without their office boys. These fears now seem to have been excessive. But of course there must, at any time, be some genuine limit. Fortunately, as income increases, the limit is pushed further and further away.

In deciding how much to spend directly on education, a government usually proceeds to aim at a standard based on a typical individual. It sets a target. This may be too ambitious, and for sheer fiscal reasons the minimum set, though generally acclaimed to be desirable, is regarded as for the time being impracticable. There was the target written into the Indian Constitution of the summary abolition of illiteracy, or the target set by the British public many years ago, of raising the compulsory school-leaving age to sixteen. These targets may eventually be realized, but not in the period that was first contemplated.

There may be a fairly clear rational basis for a state to decide what minimum education should be compulsorily given to all junior members of a society. For example, it may be regarded as basic to a modernizing economy that, in principle, all its citizens are literate. In a more advanced economy, like the United States, it has been well established that students with only eight years' completed schooling are much more liable to become unemployed in later life than those with ten or twelve years' schooling. An acceptable risk may be decided, and the number of years' schooling fixed accordingly.

So far as minimal schooling is concerned, given the standards to be reached, and the costs of hiring teachers, providing classrooms (again, according to some acceptable standard), the budget can be determined on the expenditure side. It will vary from year to year for demographic reasons—past history will determine the size of the cohorts of children going through school. The standards will remain more or less fixed, but annual total expenditure will vary.

Such a provision of minimum expenditure per head (of pupils

50

going through the system) will make only a limited contribution to greater economic equality. Other factors besides the amount of formal schooling that each pupil receives affect the end-result. Each child has his own genetic endowment, his own home with its powerful influence, not only on his learning but on his motivation and his own social environment, and the less privileged boys and girls on average do worse at school than the better endowed.

In the more extreme cases, these differences show up in percentages of drop-outs. In some poorer countries, the less motivated of the rural children can hardly be brought to school for as much as four or five consecutive years. The urban children in the same countries may be more willing and able to attend.

Many critics of educational policies, whether from realism or cynicism, take the point of view that dropping out is a sufficient indication that schooling is not necessary for many children. Why should we waste money on peasants' children, it is asked, when all their lives after leaving school they will be busy in the paddy-fields, or driving the water-buffalo from one place to another? One answer is that for agriculture to become even one or two little steps more modern, peasants have to be able to read, and the additional broader but little relevant answer is that if the peasants' children mostly drop out of education, they lose their chances of dropping in on economic growth.

While many critics have clearly accepted the principle of providing education for all, up to varying levels—but nearly always including *some* secondary education—the main idea has been to promote economic growth, or to give every individual 'what he deserves', not to equalize incomes. What children deserve, or what they need in relation to their ability to profit from an exceptional opportunity, depends on their trained capacities. The notion of 'equality of opportunity' through education is often interpreted as meaning giving to each a chance to climb the career ladder of a meritocracy.

Michael Young, in his fantasy on this subject, was the first to emphasize that equality of opportunity in education would lead to a new kind of inequality.[1] He observed that members of the new meritocracy would become part of the strength of the conservatives in Britain, who would represent 'progress' and higher productivity, as against socialists who persisted in their attachment to egalitarianism. This was a shrewd summing-up of the social and educational developments of Britain in the 1950s. Similar changes took place in other European countries.

Advancement for merit, and equality of opportunity for all children entering the school system, became the basis not only for destroying the remnants of an aristocratic system based on the family but also for creating an élite of high-grade students. As Young foretold, the 1960s were to see a revulsion against this trend, and a demand for an end to all élites whatsoever, however selected.

The Western world still has not made up its mind which way it wants to resolve the educational dilemmas arising from the multiple relationships between an educational system and society as a whole. All the subjects that are debated arise from this central issue: what kind of equality (or justice) in society are we trying to achieve? The contents of school and university curricula, the length of apprenticeships, the terms and conditions of teaching appointments, the relationship of technical colleges to other tertiary institutions, the issue of comprehensive *versus* specialized secondary schools, the form and content of examinations, all give rise to questions that cannot be resolved without a social framework. The consensus on objectives has begun to work at this point, and there is an atmosphere of uncertainty.

An economist may assume that an 'ideal democratic free society' is the unspoken end to which all are striving, and that the existence of hierarchical élites in the productive structure of the economy must be regarded as a necessary evil, not a change of direction, but such assumptions are adopted with an increasing lack of conviction. They are no longer accepted as unquestionable, like the 'truths' accepted as self-evident in the American

[1] *The Rise of the Meritocracy, 1870-2033. An essay on Education and Equality* (London: Thames & Hudson, 1958; Penguin Books, 1961).

Constitution. Even the large sections of mankind who subscribe to this ideal differ among themselves as to its meaning. The East Germans refer to their state as a 'democratic republic' as do the white South Africans to theirs, and in similar terms American journalists refer to the 'democratic Western powers'. The word 'ideal' means only that the goal is general, and probably beyond human reach. 'Democratic' refers to the democracy of the dollar among Chicago-trained economists, to a liberal regime among the supporters of American Democratic Action, to a Fabian Socialist society according to Professor Meade and the more leftish British economists, to a property-owning democracy in the Institute of Economic Affairs in London, and to some form of communist regime according to the 'democrats' east of the iron curtain. It meant none of these things among the anarchists of 1968.

These are more than semantic misunderstandings. What men receive for the work they do, how far the efforts of getting themselves 'educated' so as to be proficient in a particular occupation, are rewarded in hard cash, and other practical questions, are answered partly on terms of the democratic ideals in fashion in the country where they live.

If the proper interpretation of equality of opportunity is to raise the earning power of a new educated group, then the amount to be spent can somehow be geared to anticipated returns. The best people—those with the best talents, as shown in school reports, and school examinations—will be given still more education, and their anticipated future earning power provides a basis for deciding what total should be spent on education.[1]

On the same line of argument, the second question can be answered. How should educational expenditure be distributed?

Where an extreme inequality exists between certain social groups inside an 'advanced' country—the best-known instance being the black population in the United States—it is quite clear

---

[1] See for example the last paragraph of Professor H. G. Johnson's essay on 'The Political Economy of Opulence', in *Money, Trade and Economic Growth* (London: Allen & Unwin, 1962).

that unless special measures are taken, the more backward group will never catch up or diminish the gap with the more advanced. Such special measures may include extra educational expenditure, at any rate for an immediate critical period, to offset the effects on black children of unfavourable early environment. Another even more extreme case is that of aborigine and part-aborigine children in Australia.

But how far is the principle to be extended of spending more educationally per head on backward rather than on promising pupils? A special crash programme to help to rectify a well-recognized historical injustice suffered by a particular group may be a clearly defined and acceptable provision. But are not all, or most, 'backward' children in some sense victims of their environment? Is then educational expenditure to be made, in principle, inversely proportional to the pupil's diligence and aptitude?

Some egalitarians seem to come perilously near to adopting this position. They take their stand on Tawney's view that offering an opportunity to rise for talented students is no substitute for the general diffusion of the means of civilization to all, since this is needed by all, even if by choice, or through lack of some quality like ambition, they do not 'rise' in society. If this principle is extended to provide not only the 'means of civilization' but extra coaching and tuition to the backward, it seems that the policy has to be quantified for particular cases, and cannot be elevated into a general principle.

In an absolutely static economy, some such policy might just conceivably reduce the dispersion of earnings, in a given set of circumstances. It might so happen that all the clever boys and girls would progress just as far without special help as with it, and that the extra educational assistance given to the slower pupils would be so well arranged as to overcome their various inhibitions and mental blocks, and turn out much more productive, as well as happier citizens. Incomes might or might not become less widely dispersed, depending on the supply and demand situation for the various categories of skilled and unskilled labour. But certainly greater welfare might have been achieved than if the clever pupils had received the extra margin of educational expenditure otherwise available to them.

The world is economically dynamic. Rightly or wrongly, there is considerable anxiety, in regard to the immediate future, whether there will be a sufficient supply, in any given country, of 'highly qualified personnel'. No one doubts that in nearly all countries there should be available an adequate supply of suitable recruits. No country yet fully exploits its human resources since, for example, females and the children of the poor provide only partly tapped reservoirs of talent. What is in doubt is the availability of adequate training programmes and facilities at higher levels.

It is not easy to arrive at a definite view on the size of this problem. One recent conference[1] endorsed the view that it 'was absurd for society to spend considerable resources on giving 2·5 per cent of the number in each age-group the highest level of qualifications and *then allow this capital to depreciate*'. This implies a case for giving more education to those that have most already.

But, after all, education is not just absorbing a mass of knowledge, memorized from books. As the report suggests, in relation to the modern type of economy, education may be viewed 'as the process which enables an individual to withstand the inevitable changes which will occur in the relationship between what he learns and what he will be called upon to do in the world of work'. In some contexts, this would have to be regarded as a very narrow view, but it is relevant to a dynamic economic situation. Education over the lifetime of the individual may be needed to satisfy many ends. One narrow, but substantial purpose, is to educate all individuals in such a way as to guide the economy on a path that is consistent with the maximum attainable rate of growth.

It is not clear how many additional individuals need further training over and above what is already available. The report of

[1] OECD, *Policy Conference on Highly Qualified Manpower* (Paris, 1967).

the OECD conference[1] pointed out how difficult it was to assess this need. Investigations in Britain and the United States had suggested quite explicitly that the economic indications were that a steady equilibrium existed in both countries in the (more or less open) market for highly trained personnel. A substantial rise in the level of salaries for such personnel had not been observed in the early 1960s, as might well have been expected had there been a persistent deficit. The rate of return on expenditure on higher tertiary education, so far as it could be estimated in both countries, seemed to be less than the corresponding return on secondary education. Apart from the US and the UK it was observed that, in many countries, graduates tended to show quite high unemployment rates after completion of higher studies. Purely economic indications, therefore, for what they were worth, did not confirm the need for a greatly expanded programme.

However, for a select number, continuing higher education, broadly defined, seemed to be both needed and demanded. Expenditure showed that it was those who had received the best training for their work, who were themselves 'most keen' to take advantage of facilities for still further education. To the extent that this demand existed, there were strong arguments for satisfying it.

This is precisely why a dilemma arises. For, contrary to the special pleading sometimes advanced by businessmen, or business-school salesmen, continuous education for adults is far from cheap. It is, as the OECD report itself observed, often two or three times as costly as normal full-time university education of the same duration. This is because the earnings foregone by more senior men are much higher than the foregone earnings that can be imputed to younger students. Moreover, the average duration in a given business of the careers of men released for advanced technical courses, or higher managerial studies, is curtailed by the courses themselves and by the increasing industrial mobility of the participants. Only very large firms can afford the rising costs.

[1] Op. cit., p. 27.

The plea for 'continuing education' has to be accepted if economies are to grow. But clearly advanced courses provide for a relatively small élite, and to the extent that such programmes are carried out, they work against equality. They are designed to give to a few even better opportunities than they have had before; by their very costliness some further training programmes must tend to be made available to a carefully selected few. Expanding the programmes in various ways is possible, but, while some expansion might double the size of a particular élite group in ten years, it would not alter the fact that only a small percentage of all possible candidates for higher posts would in fact be trained.

There is a similar case to be made for 'education throughout working life' at much lower levels than that of top management. Schemes of this kind, when implemented, would introduce again a relatively small percentage of higher-trained personnel at various levels in the industrial hierarchy. Such schemes could help individuals and groups to rise, but would scarcely reduce the differential skills between groups as a whole. Inevitably, some would remain outside the training and re-training schemes, and mobility would be enhanced.[1]

Education, while it removes some reasons for inequality, increases the possibility that others will arise. A given programme may remove illiteracy, but for the first time make possible the self-development of a skilled engineer. Another programme may make available university degrees to twice as many people as previously could gain them, at the cost of inducing some profession to close its ranks against non-graduates.

There are thus serious difficulties in a dogma that asserts, in the name of equality, that expenditure should never be allowed to

[1] Professor Richard Stone of Cambridge, using a model originated by Christian von Weizsäcker of Heidelberg, shows that, if it is allowed that knowledge itself has a significant rate of obsolescence (and that it may in any case be partly forgotten over time), then re-education may be more useful to the economy, if not to the individual, than an extended provision of initial education (see papers relating to the OECD, Scientific Affairs Conference of March 1966).

create or support élites, but should rather be used directly to bring people up to as nearly as possible the same level of education. This may be called 'the fallacy of the direct approach'. The shortest way to attain the most egalitarian society that is in fact viable, with genuine chances of survival, may be precisely to channel a sufficient amount of educational expenditure into the education of economic leaders and innovators.

The Educational Dilemma and the Student Revolution
From the year 1969 onwards, the magnitude of the educational dilemma will become clearer; the preceding demographic changes, and the income of the 1960s, have made it certain that in the 1970s the size of the demand for more education—lengthening full-time and part-time courses at a variety of levels—will grow at exponential rates. Many ways of presenting the statistics are being used, but in all variants they agree on this point. At present, even in so-called 'advanced' industrial countries, a high percentage even of males in their late teenage years received no full-time education. This must change, and a shift of a few points in the percentages will double the demand for full-time education after a short interval. The dilemma is how to make these changes. For simultaneously, as the obsolescence rate of information increases—and this becomes more widely recognized—part-time education throughout life will be demanded. With scarce resources, only a new élite is likely to be educated in these new ways, although one that grows in size.

Nor is it certain along what lines the dilemma will be resolved. Some outcomes, however, are clear. The changing of the size of the universities and technical schools in Britain and other countries since 1960 has had a noticeable effect on their organization and their stability. It can hardly be doubted that the still greater changes in the demands that will be made on all institutions of tertiary (and higher secondary) instruction in the 1970s and 1980s will have an even profounder effect. What is predictable is that the institutions we now know will not survive. Their organization, style and character will utterly change. Those conservatives who regret the changes that have already occurred can, if they are fairly young, confidently if gloomily, expect even more fundamental upheavals in future.

The student revolution has already begun. Some might date it as a world-wide phenomenon from the year 1968. Earlier political activity by post-World War II students had been seen in Japan, South America, Egypt and several other countries. Far more countries saw student action in 1968, some of it violent although fatal casualties were low. There were many factors causing these outbreaks, not all of them arising from the internal frictions within existing educational institutions.

A major factor in both the Japanese and Australian student movements was the war in Vietnam, and the American Government's attitude towards this war up to the date of President Johnson's resignation. There were, too, other political pressures, and social and psychological conditions that affected the timing of the unrest. In this chapter, our concern is with the internal factors, difficulties or pressures arising from within the organizational structures of the universities and colleges.

These may be grouped under several headings. First there was the change in size itself; secondly, pressure on both research and teaching results at the same time; thirdly, the obsolescence of knowledge; fourthly, the time lag in adjusting institutions in which most appointments are made on a life-time basis; and finally, the effects of the mass media and other extra-curricular agents on the younger generation. These ought to be considered not only to establish what the historical record really is, but also because every one of these influences may be still more powerful in future.

In a study of these factors, and either their separate or joint effects on students' attitudes and actions, the implication must not be made that a reform of a few items would easily have forestalled student unrest from 1968 onwards. As already stated, there were other causes at work, which changes and concessions could not possibly have counteracted, and there were differences in objectives which were bound, sooner or later, to lead to a clash of wills. The student perhaps wanted to be trained for a new society of one kind or another, but none of their subjective utopias fell within the range of the most liberal imagination among older teachers.

On top of all these misunderstandings comes the first factor of the 1970s, that of size. The percentage of young people taking full-time education at ages 17, 18 and 19, were still quite low in the late 1960s, even in the industrialized countries, and lower still in the developing economies. Since economic growth has been found to be closely connected with the development of 'human capital', it has become inconceivable that either group of countries will allow the situation to persist; the industrialized countries are constantly trying to raise their sights to a higher growth-rate target, and the developing countries are politically committed to development.

A political factor arises in this situation—the consequences of an *absence* of higher education may be that there are costs to bear. It is difficult for any reasonably well-educated person to imagine what it would be like to have little capacity to read or learn, or to enter the modern world untrained in any skill. Yet this is what the majority of young citizens still do, even in Britain or Germany. How they survive, without breakdowns due to frustrations, in a world of moon-flights and electronics, is hard to understand; their jobs must often be menial or repetitive and dull. Their entertainment must constantly remind them of the rewards available to the more skilled in the community from whose ranks they are excluded, or in some cases, have excluded themselves, which is even more galling.

The unskilled may constitute a political danger, if no adequate means of communication between the skilled and themselves is established. The more compassionate among the skilled may seek ways to cure or mitigate the brutal dullness of the unskilleds' universe. The revolutionaries go further, and demand in the name of social justice, that standards should be suspended.

The point is that even if reforms of these matters are fully adopted, they will give rise to further problems. The percentage of an age group (say the 20-year-olds) proceeding with higher education has only to be raised from, say, 5 to 10 per cent, for the effective demand to be doubled. In states where all costs are met by state funds, this must happen, unless budgetary stringencies dictate a change of policy.

This huge increase in the numbers of full-time students will directly impinge on teaching facilities in many tertiary establishments, universities of all levels, technical colleges and art schools. This places a burden on teaching staff that will be difficult to meet. The trouble is that teaching at tertiary level is closely linked with research and higher studies. Without such higher studies, without a deeply committed involvement in the pursuit of knowledge, few teachers can inspire their pupils with the motivation to continue with *their* studies. Teachers need 'research' and depend upon its prosecution.

The adult world needs research, too, for the benefits that new knowledge can confer. Resources are being poured into universities and technical colleges to support or extend research institutes of many kinds. The best personnel available for lecturing or teaching are liable to be attracted away by the rival charms of research.

The tertiary institutions are likely to see an unending, and in some ways disconcerting, struggle for funds between those who advocate better teaching and those who want more research results. The need for research will grow greater, not less, the more that is in fact successfully accomplished. Research feeds on itself. If a particular range of knowledge is made spectacularly obsolescent by one set of discoveries, a whole set of ranges of knowledge in adjacent areas becomes suspect, and has to be investigated. A breakthrough in one field leads to a programme of enquiry in neighbouring fields that has to be carried out.

Rapid obsolescence of knowledge has grave consequences for teaching programmes. The most obvious impact is on the syllabus. This has to be frequently redesigned and rewritten from start to finish, so that new theorems can be fitted into existing courses. But there are wider consequences. Students who

61

have successfully completed an up-to-date course in, say, physics or mechanics, find themselves thinking in terms which perhaps none of their future employers really understand, even though few would admit it. The present young person graduating from a course will find himself to be obsolescent in fifteen or twenty years if he makes no attempt to carry on with an 'all-life' self-educational policy. More courses for adults will be continually required, despite their high economic cost to society. Successful research will increase, not diminish, the pressure on teachers, and create additional demands on their time.

One kind of research may have some contrary, and therefore favourable, effects, and that is research into methods of teaching and learning. Present methods, while some are successful, have been based mainly upon common sense and tradition, reliable enough pillars in an unchanging world. But to meet the new challenge that is coming, more should be known systematically about the effectiveness of various teaching methods. Answers have to be found, too, to the unanswered question: what is education?

Whatever it is and, no doubt, the widely received opinion on this will differ over the generations—time is needed to bring tertiary institutions into line with any new requirements. Even in a highly rational society, decisions on courses would take time to be reached; many interests and points of view have to be considered before a university or a technical college drafts and accepts a proposed new subject. After agreement has been reached, and the plan adopted at the appropriate administrative level, there is a further time lag while a new department is created or an old one suitably enlarged. Nor is the actual procedure followed ever wholly rational. Tertiary educational institutions, like other human organizations, are scenes of rivalries, jealousies, emotional attachments and ambitions, and no 'ploy' is better established than the 'reference back' to a consultative committee. Often a proposal when it first appears is indeed badly thought out, and open to some legitimate criticisms. But, in practice, criticism is often indulged in for other reasons than to find the objectively most valid solution.

This is not the place to examine the reasons for the top-heavy inefficiencies that plague most educational institutions. Since autocracy is out of fashion, they are run on the basis of a special version of democracy that allows nearly all staff members a right to participate in decision-forming. Those outside the list of participants are nowadays often clamouring to get in. A bureaucracy of administrators controls the machinery of meetings. As able and critical individuals are often tertiary-grade teachers, they provide a group professionally biased towards debate and disagreement, and averse to makeshift compromises or political deals. Whatever the ultimate reasons, most academic governing bodies, and their sub-committees, are mostly time-wasting and inefficient.

Academics in general tend to despise the mass media. It is from their houses that television is excluded most frequently. As a group they do not take popular newspapers, and many academics confine their reading of news to a few items in a conservative daily paper. Most students have been brought up under the influence of mass media, especially of television.

Television's influence on education has been both good and bad. It would seem a cliché to note that it has been very powerful, but it *is* worth noting in the light of the ignorance of so many academics about it. The point is that television's presentation of a man, as a person or as a politician, or its portrayal and discussion of a current event, may be fair and interesting, or prejudiced and dull, or some other mixture of these attributes. What hardly ever happens is that the television contributions leave things quite unchanged. Once its impact is made it is not very easily unmade.

Television is also the greatest educational medium the world has yet seen, and, as this is widely recognized (outside some university circles), many are using it to educate. But, of course, the motives of the hidden educators are numberless and difficult to ascertain.

The educational dilemma will have to be resolved somehow in the 1970s, in a world profoundly changed by all these factors.

The educational system in any country contributes to greater equality, to the extent that it reduces the disparities in relative earnings, particularly by raising the economic value of the un-skilled or lowest-paid workers; it contributes to inequality by sharpening the absolute differences between the higher grades of skilled. This, at least, is a plausible hypothesis based on general observation and fairly close economic analysis.

When the student revolutionaries attack society as a whole they may or may not succeed in destroying or changing it; when they attack simply the educational establishments with all their ramifications, they have little hope of lasting success. Some inequalities allegedly linked to education, such as those that arose from restriction of entry to the medical and legal pro-fessions, result from deliberately organized imperfections in the labour market. They are similar, in principle, to other restrictions on entry, such as that exercised by the printing and other craft unions. Such imperfections of the market can be modified or reduced under pressure from students or other political activists.

But other inequalities are much harder to remove, nor is it clear that they should be removed. They may fall well within that ideal of a 'reasonable degree of inequality' that is wholly justified as contributing to a successful and viable society.

In a free labour market, higher wages would be paid for a skilled than for an unskilled man because his marginal product was higher. Supposing that, to attain a given level of skill, a man needs to undergo a period of training. This will entail a direct cost, and an indirect opportunity cost due to his foregoing some income during the training period. The two together are the total cost of training. He will be acting rationally to incur this cost if he can anticipate, with some certainty, that his later additional earnings justify his current expenditure on training.[1]

The higher the return on his training outlay that a man is likely to gain, the more strongly motivated he will be to take that training. If no training whatever were available, the abler in-

[1] His later earnings, say W_{ts}, integrated over his earning life and dis-counted back to the present, must exceed W_{tu}, treated in the same way, by C, the cost of training (when W_{tu} is the level of 'untrained' earnings).

64

dividuals could still often expect to earn more than the less able. Ability takes many forms, and there would be no exact correlation between all definitions of a man's capacity, but it is likely that the man who in general had greater intelligence and organizing power could anticipate earning more than the man with less, education apart. This very fact would also be consistent with the 'able' man expecting a greater return on educational outlay than the less 'able' man. This would be an average result and not without exceptions.

The unfortunate consequence for equality is that it tends to be the abler men who get the greater training, so long as training and education are geared to the market for skills. They take this additional training precisely because they anticipate substantially greater earnings.

Even in a socialist society, so long as outputs and services are rationally valued, the same result would occur. There would need to be a differential in earnings, if only to allocate labour resources to the best uses, in a rationally conducted socialist economy—and even if most of the differentials were taxed away subsequently. In practice, most socialist economies have introduced substantial differentials (and have *not* taxed them away completely). It is the demand for highly skilled persons that creates the supply. Whether the choice is made mainly by the individual, or by the state, the cost of education is increased and incurred more heavily for the able man than for the less able, precisely because they are the best scarce material for educational processing.

CHAPTER 4

FORCES IN SOCIETY THAT PROMOTE EQUALITY

Statisticians have established that, in the United States and some other industrialized economies, there has been some reduction in inequality of income over the first half of the twentieth century, both before and after tax. On the whole, as average income has risen, dispersion of incomes has lessened. It seems that greater equality is easier to attain in the richer than in the poorer countries.

In the case of Great Britain, pre-tax income distribution for the mid-1960s plotted on a Lorenz curve show some reduction in inequality since 1949 from the middle income upwards, while there seems to have been little change for the lower-income group. On a Lorenz diagram, if every income earner had the same income (perfect equality), the cumulative distribution would follow a 45 degree diagonal straight line. With one man appropriating all the national income, the curve would approximate closely to the horizontal (0 to 100 per cent) of incomes and the right-hand vertical (100 to 100 per cent). The progressive reduction in inequality of incomes is depicted by a slight movement in the upper part of the curve, over time, towards the diagonal.

There are serious statistical difficulties in the way of comparing pre-war and post-war income distributions even for countries with comprehensive statistical services. This is because income-tax has varied over long periods very substantially. Since, to construct a Lorenz curve, a reasonably accurate estimate of the number of incomes is required, and a very large but uncounted number lay below the tax exemption limit, in earlier years, this method of comparison is not always reliable. Similar difficulties of coverage arise in using Lorenz curves for international comparisons. Statisticians have, therefore, had recourse to other methods, no single one of which is the most satisfactory for all ranges of income or for all comparisons.

The Lorenz curves are usually found to be best for visual comparisons, if and when the data of the periods or places concerned are reasonably comparable in scope. For middle- and upper-income groups the Pareto curve gives useful results, especially if interpolations are wanted (for instance, an estimate of the number of incomes lying between two income levels not directly given in the data). Another useful method is to calculate other percentile incomes, for instance, what percentage of total taxable income accrues to the top 1 per cent, or bottom 10 per cent, of income recipients. These calculations can be made for a number of countries at different dates.[1]

Political pressures may have largely accounted for the improved post-tax distribution of incomes, but other forces must have determined the egalitarian tendency in pre-tax receipts. These cannot be precisely determined or measured but they certainly include the following:

1. Increasing scarcity of labour in relation to demand, itself partly due to the progressive removal of young people from the labour market, and direct legislative activity, have abolished low wages as a major cause of poverty.

2. Full employment policies followed (to a varying extent) by most governments since 1945 have removed a large part of the impact of low levels of employment on earnings as a whole.

3. Big shifts in the 'skill-mix' of the labour force have continuously taken place. Most movements of labour force from one set

---

[1] So far as Great Britain is concerned, the clearest review of these points is in R. J. Nicholson's *Economic Statistics and Economic Problems* (McGraw-Hill, 1969), Chapter 8, and in the same author's article in the *Lloyd's Bank Review*, Jan. 1967. Harold Lydall's comprehensive *The Structure of Earnings* (Oxford: Clarendon Press, 1968) gives a thorough review of methods and of available international comparisons, calculated by himself. *The Distribution of National Income* (London: Macmillan, 1968) edited by Jean Marchal and Bernard Ducros, contains a number of articles relevant to these problems of measurement, and also to the problems of income.

changes in inequality
move towards equality ?

of occupations to another have been upwards, in skill and in pay.
4. Wider educational provision, at less than cost to the recipient,
has tended to equalize earnings, by increasing the supply of manpower into many of the skilled categories.
5. Technological changes that have linked material economic
growth to the internal mass markets have played a part. If
prosperity depends not upon selling 10,000 hand-painted china
tea-sets to upper middle class gentlewomen, but rather on selling
ten million tea-cups to works canteens and offices, then real
incomes will tend to become applied to finance the opportunity.

Will these forces persist, so compelling the equalizing process
to continue, or will there be a relapse under one or more of these
heads? Will the economic tendencies working for greater equalization spread to the developing countries, or have they, as is often
predicted, a pre-take-off period of greater inequality to go
through?
The first of the economic factors making for greater economic
equality in society is the increase in the scarcity of labour.
Scarcity is a relative term, not only as between one economy and
another, but as between labour, land and capital. An equal
amount of labour can be relatively scarce if it is joined with
plentiful land or a plentiful supply of capital. The countries where
labour has often become scarce historically are the new countries
like the western parts of the United States, Australia and Canada, or
the planned economies that have provided substantial real capital
by deliberate policy. When the new countries were being settled,
land was available even for working-men without capital, if
they were prepared for the hard life of a homesteader or squatter.
In these conditions wages tended to be high, by the standards of
the time. This stimulated the employers to organize work carefully, so that labour output should not be wastefully used and
to invent and adopt labour-saving machinery. The frontier's
contribution to progress were the sewing machine, and the
threshing machine, as well as the Colt revolver and Winchester
rifle, on which its expansive imperialism throve. In the planned

68

economies, intensive industrialization policies presumably raised the demand for labour sufficiently to absorb labour leaving agriculture, as well as a growing work force.

It is not possible, however, to identify with certainty all the forces at work that have promoted a relatively greater equality of incomes. So far as earned incomes are concerned, for those countries which have records,[1] it appears that New Zealand and Australia, Czechoslovakia and Hungary were typically in the group of relatively low dispersion. Two of these were countries of pioneer settlement over the last 150 years, and some of the forces of economic and social equalization which have been mentioned would, no doubt, have been at work. The other two are planned socialist economies, neither of them large. It may be surmised that a high level of employment, a considerable amount of central planning (removing the need for high-level executives throughout the system), and a deliberate policy of educational expansion have also been among the factors promoting relative equalization in economies of this type.

Some of the developing countries were to be found at the other end of the spectrum. In Lydall's group of twenty-five countries, Brazil, Chile, India, Ceylon and Mexico stood out as the five with high inequality. From this it may reasonably be concluded that dispersion of pre-tax income is in some degree inversely related to economic development, although other factors are clearly at work. The most developed countries, like the USA or Sweden, might otherwise have been at the head of the list instead of in a second group, of fairly low dispersion. At least, it is not unduly optimistic to hope that as economic development takes place, in the long run dispersion will become noticeably less extreme.

Beyond this prediction, it is very difficult to go. The national output of a country has to be distributed between a number of heterogeneous claimants. The largest group is identified in the statistics as 'households', a title which may well cover a different

[1] Twenty-five countries were compared by Harold Lydall in report of percentiles of his 'standard distribution' of earned incomes (op. cit., Tables 5-6, p. 156).

set of social arrangements from one decade to the next. Households receive income either for personal services or as a return on property owned. Some income is retained as profits by business firms (corporations or companies) or by governments, in their various capacities as providers of services, and some income, in a given period, goes directly to governmental recipients as taxes.

Professor Kuznets has calculated that in twelve developed countries, in the years 1954-60, on average the service and property income of households totalled 74.2 per cent of the gross national product.[1] The rest of the national product, to which interest on the public debt has to be added, covered net indirect taxes, capital consumption, and corporate earnings and taxes.

The 74·2 per cent was composed of employee compensation (which was 50·6 per cent of GNP), the income of entrepreneurs and the property income of households. Thus only half of gross national product went directly to employees in wages and salaries. An analysis of earned income covers only this part of receipts.

Personal income is a bigger proportion of gross national product, since this includes not only the income of households (74·2 per cent), but also money transfers to households (pensions and transfers of all kinds), and the value to households of government fixed services. For 1954-60, personal income was 88·2 per cent of gross product.

Employee compensation can evidently be changed not only by raising the gross national product but by diminishing the share of that product going to some of the other claimants. If an increase in employee compensation were effected in this way, it might or might not increase the degree of equalization in the society, depending upon which other claimants suffered, and which sector of earners received most benefit. The long-term trend has been for the compensation of employees to rise in developed countries, in the twentieth century, as compared with distribution at the end of the nineteenth, in relation to the income going to property, or that going to entrepreneurs and self-employed recipients. On the other hand, the rise in transfer incomes, which

[1] Simon Kuznets, *Modern Economic Growth* (Yale Univ. Press, 1966).

has had, on the whole, an equalizing tendency, has tended to keep down the proportion going to households for current economic services while sustaining or raising the proportion of all personal income.

In terms of 'distributive shares', that is the shares in the national income of employees, entrepreneurs and self-employed, and asset-owners, in the United Kingdom and United States, the first group, employees, were receiving 69 per cent or 70 per cent by the period 1954-60, as against some 47-54 per cent nearly a hundred years earlier. The income from assets was only 19-21 per cent (as against 36 per cent in the UK in 1860-9), and the income of entrepreneurs and self-employed was down to 9-12 per cent. In France and Germany, where prosperous (if subsidized) peasant agriculture, and small-scale retailing and even manufacturing, were still relatively common, this last item still stood as high as 22 per cent (Germany) and 29 per cent (France), but even in these countries the percentage of national income going to employees was up to some 60 per cent.

The share of income going as a return on assets seems to have followed varying patterns in different countries, especially after the First World War. Since World War II it has declined in a number of countries (including Belgium, Norway, Japan, Australia and New Zealand). The fraction of total assets held by corporations or governments, rather than by self-employed persons or individual enterpreneurs, has undoubtedly risen considerably, and this is a most important change.

So far as economists are concerned, the rise in the developed countries of the share of employee compensation is explained by a rise in the price per man-hour of labour (since weekly hours worked has declined), in comparison with the price per unit (however defined) of capital services. The shortening in the working week has itself, no doubt, contributed to greater efficiency per man-hour, but not in a sufficient degree to be a major explanation of the change. A greater expenditure on education is the other factor that has contributed to greater efficiency. Here it would be wrong to think in terms either of formal education

71

alone, or of specific skills, although there has been an improvement in both. In addition, the whole environment of social life in advanced countries has completely changed, raising the extent of communication between human groups in a revolutionary manner; more than once, in the last few decades, there have been inflexions in this curve. The coming of the cinema, and of the motor-bus serving country as well as urban areas, changed the outlook and capabilities of millions of people, over and above the direct contributions of schools and colleges. Radio, television, paperback editions of books and aeroplane travel have made their own impact in the last few decades.

Not only have employees become a bigger proportion of the total labour force in the developed countries, than they were sixty or a hundred years ago, but their income per head has risen in relation to the income per head of entrepreneurs and the self-employed. The increased productivity of the economy has risen from factors which economists were slow to forecast. The 'residual', as it came to be called, was more important than increases in either capital or labour, in the growth of economies. The coefficients of any supposed production function kept changing, fortunately for the better. Economies of scale (which include economies of specialization made possible by expanding markets, and are not therefore a simple function of size of plant), and other sources of improved efficiency, not all of them even yet fully identified or understood, have allowed labour to gain an ever increased real reward from the economic system.

Among the factors that have, as it has turned out, promoted greater equality in the modern industrial economies, must be counted the forces for greater efficiency of output that have so noticeably, and largely unpredictably, affected their changing industrial structure. Instead of diminishing returns to scale, economies as a whole have shown ever-increasing returns. Technological change has been one basic cause of this phenomenon. The whole outlook in regard to such change is as different as it could be from the pessimistic view that was held about it only thirty or forty years ago, when stagnation was feared on every side.

In Britain, a typical and persuasive representative of a conservative view was Hubert Henderson, who vehemently maintained that industrial growth in the nineteenth century was a 'once off' performance, due to the opening up of the American frontier and other familiar factors of nineteenth-century international trade. In his view no such rates of growth could come again because no similar frontiers existed or could be found. Yet in the 1950s Britain grew faster than in any previous decade and new 'frontiers' of expansion were found throughout the world.[1] Keynes was impatient with the idea that investment opportunities were petering out, but his references to the Pyramids, or to the rebuilding of South London, were thought at the time to be almost reductions to the absurd, and Hicks ended his famous book[2] with a footnote to the effect that all modern European growth might have been a single—and

[1] For instance, Henderson referred to international investment in the nineteenth century as 'the main lubricant of an automatic, self-adjusting system', and thought in 1943 that international investment would not again (after World War II) be of the same type. In the Stamp Memorial lecture of 1946, Henderson referred to the 'untapped resources in the hinterlands of new continents being opened up' in the nineteenth century, and the 'grand international division of labour' of that period's 'freely working economic system . . . regulated only by impersonal economic laws'. This he contrasted with the between-the-World-Wars period as follows: 'Whereas international trade had previously led the way in the process of expansion, and helped everything forward, it now lagged behind and held everything else back.' Henderson quite prophetically remarked of the future that 'the most difficult economic problems for the world, and by far the greatest for this country, will be the international problems'. But his prediction was founded on two mistaken assumptions, based on inter-war precedent: first, he thought that the rate of population increase would decline further, and secondly, that the failure of the volume of international trade (and in particular of British exports) to expand was a 'serious possibility'. Henderson showed great wisdom, however, in stressing the serious long-term character of the imbalance likely to arise for British overseas trade and in advocating the consideration of quantitative controls of imports until this imbalance was overcome. (See *The Inter-War Years and other Papers* (Oxford Univ. Press, 1955, pp. 257, 377 et. seq.)
[2] *Value and Capital.*

73

doomed to end—response to a flash-in-the-pan population explosion cycle. In the USA Hansen, himself a natural optimist, for a while propounded the possibility of stagnation.

At the present time, technology is seen as to all intents and purposes limitless in scope. Problems may arise to which technology would have no direct answer, but there is more readiness to change the problem, and to look for goals that are realizable. Nor is the notion anywhere entertained that technological improvement will come to a halt, or even slow down very much. Whether rightly or wrongly, the current assumption most widely held is that, given sufficient expenditure, almost any technical 'bottleneck' to growth can be broken or circumvented. Even if this assumption proves one day to have been too sanguine in a particular direction, there is much evidence to justify its use over most of our thinking.

Today the economic and social problems are seen to be just *that*, not to be problems in the sphere of technology. There is now no nagging fear that methods of production and expansion will reach a point beyond which they cannot be much improved, or that markets will fail because people will be satiated with goods—another phantom of the 1930s. The graver dangers are social, political and moral.

The rise in the rewards of employees can be repeated in developing countries in the same way as has occurred in the developed, provided that the social and economic structures of these countries can be adapted to change. There is no doubt that, partly in response to economic changes which neither the orthodox economists nor the Marxists predicted, political claims have been made by workers, in various categories, and that in consequence their general conditions have improved. Some would give credit to the political activities of union and labour parties for the economic improvement, and no doubt there has been some cause and effect working both ways. But the agitations would have had no lasting victories if economic change, based on underlying production possibilities, had not been favourable. The question is whether the same set of forces will work towards equalization in the newly developing countries, and, indeed, what will happen in the more developed parts of the world, and what, above all, will be a satisfactory relationship between these changing areas.

The New Industrial Order

Some twenty years after the announcement of a 'managerial revolution', there appeared a new analysis of the industrial 'technostructure'; after Burnham came Galbraith—the Galbraith of 1967,[1] not the price controller or the ambassador to India. Slogans from his book were used by French students in the events of 1968 to liven up the turgid pronouncements of Marcuse. What was this new technostructure, named by Galbraith and given plausibility by his pen? It was no longer the managers, according to Galbraith—if it ever had been—who took the key decisions in industry; such decisions nowadays depended upon such complex considerations that the effective power had to be 'lodged deeply' down inside the large organizations, and to be made by a conglomeration of the technical, planning and other specialized staff of those organizations—this staff would be called the technostructure.

The power of the technostructure was greater than that of the preceding 'managers', or that of the competing capitalist owners of yesteryear, who had run their own small business themselves in direct and simple competition with each other. Nowadays, typical business was big business, and it decided not only how goods should be produced, but what goods should be produced and it then set itself the task of creating markets, and persuading the public that they needed the things which the technostructure reckoned could be made and sold economically. The technostructure so described may perhaps be regarded as the creation more of the caricaturist than of the portrait painter, but there is some element of truth at least, as applied to the American scene and to business all over the world where it is modelled

[1] See J. H. Galbraith, *The New Industrial State* (London: Hamish Hamilton, 1967).

on the American pattern, in this picture of a now controlling oligarchy.

What are the goals and aims of the technostructure? For Galbraith this question was of great significance, since he had adopted the axiom that members of social groups have their own goals, and tend to pursue those goals to the exclusion of all others. To the extent that a technostructure, if it really exists, pursues self-interest, it will surely promote inequality, for it must be in a strong position to improve its own material advantage to the detriment of the rest of the public. But Galbraith was not content to accept so commonplace a view. For him, the important point was precisely the opposite. According to his view of the technostructure, it must be working within a definite set of constraints and inhibitions. Its members would spurn naked selfishness and would not applaud tricks by individuals to steal marches on each other. There are, in Galbraith's view, four possible incentives for work: 1 compulsion (as under slavery), 2 compensation (wages or salaries), 3 identification (of the employee with the organization for which he works), and 4 'adaptation', a similar sense of identification made wider by a desire to conform.

If Galbraith is right, the technostructure tends to operate with motives (3) and (4). Any member of it would repudiate the suggestion that he worked for an extra half-hour or more at night, after the office was closed, merely to gain more cash. He would work long hours out of 'interest in the problem', or for 'the good of the firm'. If this interpretation is correct, one consequence is, Galbraith points out, that there is no *a priori* reason why the decision-makers should have as their goal the maximization of the return to capital. A more likely hypothesis is that they will want to maximize something else, the success of the organization (however that is conceived), or the size of the operation. The technostructure does not supply capital, nor does it even supply 'management' in a narrow sense, and therefore it will not maximize capital or managerial returns. It supplies talent and organization of multiple kinds, and will presumably seek to consolidate its power and maximize the rewards, some material but some immaterial, received in the exercise of its powers.

Would this mean greater or less inequality in the system? To answer this it would be necessary to go further than a hypothesis, and actually to find out empirically what the different 'technostructures' were doing. It would also be necessary to note that the technostructure has a considerable say in how the economic rewards to production are, in actual fact, distributed. The behaviour of the decision-makers, though not the only factor to consider, must be a major determinant of rewards.

To the extent that technostructures are a modernizing form of organization, they are more likely to be found in new, technically efficient, large industries than in old, obsolescent and small enterprises, and are therefore likely to be willing to pay high rewards for work well done. A time may come when these forms themselves are superseded, but in the meantime, and within the limits imposed by the need to safeguard their own interests, they will tend to be 'progressive employers'.

The whole question of how modern managers are to be trained and supplied to industry is still unsolved. In general, the answer must be in terms of more adequate education, but what kinds of education are appropriate, and how they should be supplied are problems in themselves. Business and management courses, widely used in the United States, were begun extensively in Britain in the 1960s. Surveys of the undergraduates taking these courses have tended to emphasize the point that the types attracted to them tend to be more motivated by the prospect of high material rewards than by any other consideration! If they intend to join the technostructure it is for compensation rather than for 'adaptation'. Least of all, are the British entrants to these courses concerned with public welfare or any other altruistic motive.

It would hardly be surprising if Continental, European and even American students tended, over the next ten years, to relapse back into non-altruism. This reaction may be hard-boiled, but it would be consistent with a swing against the petulance, irresponsibility and intolerance of some left-wing demonstrators.

77

In any case, it hardly seems to be likely that the technostructure would, at present, sponsor or support any strong campaign to reduce inequality significantly.

But there is another possibility inherent in the situation that has been reached. If Galbraith's suggestion is right, 'adaptation' is a more powerful motive than compensation. It appeals to a more integrated personality. Monetary rewards in a competitive society are like badges or medals. In America there always has been, and still is, a more widely recognized acceptance of what may be called the ethic of the almighty dollar. Many Americans in responsible professional or business jobs incline to the belief that a man has a moral duty to earn as much as he can, without overstepping any laws beyond some socially acceptable limit. This belief may be found in all acquisitive societies, but it certainly is easier to discover in America.

This belief has come to be questioned everywhere. There has always been a steady undercurrent of criticism to it, welling up in sentimental form in the daydreams popularized by the mass media (cartoon strips extolling people with hearts of gold rather than high bank balances, or films of honest yokels pitchforked to Washington to remind a sophisticated capital of the primitive American virtues). This opposition has taken on recently a more strident note. Now that the standard of living has risen so much, there is an appreciation, or a suspicion, even—or especially— among the successful members of a materialistic society, that this world's possessions are not alone a proof of merit. Other rewards are needed.

All societies have, of course, stopped short of succumbing exclusively to the materialistic creed. Side by side with high incomes and capital gains have been medals, mayors' or sheriffs' offices, honours, or grand-masterships, in the Freemasons or some other order, titles (in some countries), or honorary degrees. The very existence of this second parallel set of recognitions of merit supports the idea that the almighty dollar system, effective over a wide range, leaves ungalvanized some of the deeper ambitions of some very active citizens.

As the average standard of life has risen, so the distinction of having rather more than enough to eat, if one so wishes, better housing and a freer command over both conspicuous and inconspicuous luxuries has become much less striking, and less satisfying. Many studies have shown that reward rather than punishment is more effective in influencing behaviour. The question at issue is what kinds of reward are most effective in influencing the behaviour of educated and sophisticated men. The answer is not likely to be simple, and may vary from decade to decade, and from one society to another. It is a not improbable hypothesis that men will be most highly motivated by appeals to the highest ideals, and deepest instincts (to use nineteenth-century language) that they possess. Fear of annihilation of oneself and one's own social group, loyalty to one's nation, pride in one's unit, have proved in many wars and confrontations to provide powerful motive forces. As far as economists are concerned, this is 'where we came in'; David Hume and Adam Smith began the great debate on motivation by asking themselves what possible motive could be found to substitute for those powerful drives that had activated a sceptical people to victory in the Seven Years War, although at their nominal head was no one more charismatic than a dreary Hanoverian. The answer, cynical but objective, was private selfishness, and the doctrine of the invisible hand was then refurbished.

If, now, a deeper analysis, and longer experience make us qualify the doctrine that, by a lucky accident, private selfishness, vigorously enough pursued, will result in the greatest achievable public gain, what now is the recipe for policy? That must depend upon man's response to his present (and future) total environment. It is not enough to study overcrowded rats in cages, or octopi with half their brains cut out, illuminating though some of the contributions of psychology and zoology may be to the by-ways of behavioural response. The total environment includes world events, in so far as they impinge, with varying force, upon individuals in society. It includes power forces, desire for social recognition, family ties and inhibitions and ambitions, social

79

relationships, and many other factors in addition to the simple desire to maximize some economic variable. Precisely because relative income determination is necessarily influenced by forces that are the subject of analysis in many different academic disciplines, it is difficult to construct a theory of that determination, without naïvety over one or other stage in the argument.

For these reasons, inflation and relative incomes have become central and in a real sense insoluble social and economic problems in the advanced industrialized economies.

CHAPTER 5

INEQUALITY AND POLITICS

In a developing country like, for instance, Thailand, a reasonably successful business man, or a third- or fourth-rank foreign adviser to the Thai Government, or to a United Nations agency (of whom there are many in Bangkok) received in the 1960s a monthly salary about one hundred times that of a Thai policeman. In Western countries persons of similar occupation and social rank might receive five or six times (at the most) a policeman's pay.

With such a distribution of incomes (and Thailand is by no means an extreme example) developing countries must clearly have social and political problems quite different in scale from those in developed countries, where income dispersion is less. To stick to the policeman example, one problem is how, with these resources, to keep him, or the military, loyal to the regime and not too hopelessly corrupt. As for the business men with the high earnings, how are they going to be taxed? They are clearly in a position to oppose legislative proposals on taxation, to bribe many officials, and to evade most assessments. They cannot usually be successfully attacked head on, since they form precisely the class which the government needs to encourage if there is to be economic growth.

One of the greatest sources of inequality is a high proportion of working population in a relatively low earning occupation, like agriculture. The relationship between this kind of inequality and political stability, is very complex. It would be naïve to assert that there is, in all societies alike, a kind of flash-point, so that beyond a certain extreme an agriculturally-induced dispersion of incomes would imply inevitably what has been called 'a revolutionary situation'. A number of factors have to coincide before societies are overturned by violence, if that is

F

the only type of event to which the word 'revolution' is to be applied.

Professor Gerschenkron in a recent book[1] has quoted approvingly de Tocqueville's view that it was economic prosperity among the French peasants rather than its reverse that hastened the advent of the French revolution, an insight which Professor Gerschenkron finds to be supported by modern research. The Russian case (in 1905) was quite different, for the industrialization of Russia in the 1890s seems to have been at the expense of the peasants, unlike the French improvements of the eighteenth century. The point is that any grave disturbance of an initial social and economic balance, at however low a level, may create a revolutionary crisis. Violent change may be precipitated by prosperity especially if it is both recent and now under threat, or it may be precipitated by deepening misery.

It is not just the degree of inequality in developing societies that has to be studied, in order to predict which of them will explode, like overheated volcanoes. Much more important are the dynamics of the local situation, the class structure of the society, its regional problems, and its external relations. Moreover the type of upheaval that should be classified as a 'revolution' would need to be carefully defined.

Professor Finer has shown, in a convincing manner, that it is quite reasonable to expect that many developing countries should go through a period of army dictatorship, under a 'man on horseback', someone not just at the head of the army but with what Weber called 'charisma'.

But, of course, in the most important economic society in the world, the United States of America, the connexion between inequality of incomes and politics has recently been most strikingly demonstrated.[2] In the early 1960s the extent of poverty in America became a political issue and was made known to the non-poor

[1] *Continuity in History and Other Essays*, by Alexander Gerschenkron (Cambridge, Mass.: Harvard Univ. Press, 1968).

[2] See particularly *The Politics of Poverty*, by John C. Donovan (New York: Pegasus, 1967).

public by such widely read studies as Michael Harrington's 1962 bombshell.[1] The man who deliberately chose to make the tackling of this problem his own contribution to his country's progress and presumably to his own lasting fame, was President Lyndon B. Johnson. He had learnt under Roosevelt the importance politically of widening the outlook of his political party, as well as the basis of its popular support. Working with President Truman, Johnson had ample opportunity to study the difficulties and frustrations that a reforming President might meet both in and out of Congress. Truman's 'Fair Deal' and his beginnings of a 'medicine' programme and his integration programmes had only had a limited success.

President Johnson, with his great influence in the Congress, with his political experience and skill and with the advantage of a special 'honeymoon period' in the aftermath of John F. Kennedy's tragic assassination, was able to get through Congress all of the unfinished business of the Kennedy era. Two forces combined to make him take a further step forward. First, he needed both for political and perhaps for psychological reasons, to add to the Kennedy programme some outstanding and recognizably Johnsonian contributions of his own; and secondly one of the first great popular demonstrations of the new political era (the march on Washington of August 1963) brought home the urgent demands of the negro community for jobs and for votes. As negro votes were increasingly going to be exercised in the northern and western states and less proportionately in the South, the political pressure became increasingly severe.

Chapter Two of the 1964 Economic Report of the President gave an official account of the extent and effect of poverty in America. The problem of poverty and the problem of the negro in America are not identical but they are closely interconnected. The Economic Report showed that over 9 million families in 1962 had less than $3,000 a year and could reasonably be classified as poor. Over 11 million children were in these poor families.

[1] *The Other America: Poverty in the United States*, by Michael Harrington (New York: Macmillan, 1962).

Twenty-two per cent of the poor were non-white; nearly half of the non-whites were poor. Later studies have broadly confirmed these orders of magnitude.

The other alarming statistics that were highlighted at this time were the much higher unemployment rate among negroes than among white workers. A 4 per cent national unemployment rate implied an 8 per cent unemployment rate among negroes. For young male negroes between the ages of sixteen and twenty-one the rate was often as high as 25 per cent, while for female negroes it was 33 per cent.

What this showed beyond question was that 'full employment' as defined by the new economists (mostly Keynesians) was not enough.[1] It might be an adequate overall economic objective (to aim at 4 per cent of unemployment) but as this was consistent with so high a rate among negroes this failed to satisfy social and political objectives. For there was even some evidence that the relative position of the negroes in regard to joblessness had deteriorated since 1948.

Is it possible to solve a major social problem like the poverty issue in America without a drastic rearrangement of political power? Many observers would have answered this question negatively. Certainly when the Economic Opportunity Act of 1964 was passed by Congress, few realized what its political implications might be. This law had six Titles, the first two being the main ones relevant to the political side of the poverty campaign. Title I established three youth programmes, expanding an earlier scheme put to Senate by the Kennedy administration. Title II (which was not amended by Congress) introduced the concept of 'community action programs'.

The key clause, which was 202 (a) (3), inserted, as a definition of a community action programme, that it was one 'which is developed, conducted and administered with the max-

[1] The late Sir Hubert Henderson, in a long drawn-out controversy with Keynes himself, often pointed out the possibility that serious problems of local or structural unemployment might be overlooked if economists confined their attention to national aggregates.

imum feasible participation of residents of the areas and members of the groups served'. This does not in so many words say 'the participation of the poor', but this of course was taken to be implied.

Robert Kennedy, still Attorney-General at that time, explained the matter to the relevant House Committee as follows:

'The institutions which affect the poor—education, welfare, recreation, business, labour—are huge, complex structures, operating far outside their control . . . The community action programs must basically change these organizations by building into the program real representation of the poor. This bill calls for maximum feasible participation of residents. This means the involvement of the poor in planning and implementing programs: giving them a real voice in their institutions.'

This was undoubtedly a revolutionary proposal in one or more ways; first, because it proposed giving power to persons not yet wielding power through any existing institution, and, secondly because it cut across the bureaucracy of the city, state and even federal governments, putting a direct relationship between a central federal government agency and the local communities. In effect, this Title made it possible that federal technical assistance be made directly available to local groups of poor people, who could in effect challenge the political power of existing welfare, educational and political institutions.

The Office of Economic Opportunity was duly set up, under Mr Shriver. His office for a time at least had a fairly free hand in trying to determine what 'maximum feasible participation' was to mean in both the large and small American communities. Undoubtedly the phrase, and the concept, had been put into the bill originally by professional social experts—not by the poor— or as a result of any direct political pressure from voters. When the experts, under Shriver, tried to administer the concept they were soon in political difficulties, first from the majors of the cities, who reacted strongly against being by-passed in the handing out of funds, and secondly from other professional

85

administrators, in various federal departments and especially from those in the Bureau of the Budget.

A certain mystery remains about the development and ending of this story. How was it that so shrewd a politician as President Johnson entered on this enterprise without having assessed the opposition it would engender? And why, having set his hand to this purpose, did he allow his energies to be wholly side-tracked into another direction?

These are problems of history which may become elucidated and clarified as Johnson, and other elder statesmen of his period, publish their memoirs. Some would content themselves with pointing out that the Vietnam war became an obsession with the President which effectively seemed to drain him of energy for a strong domestic policy. Others would point to the hearty opposition from the poor themselves that Shriver ran into, since they unexpectedly ceased to be docile recipients of aid and demanded 'participation' in positive terms.

The point of Mr Donovan's story of the Johnson administration is general and not particular to America. Any programme to tackle inequalities of income on at all a serious scale must be a political programme.

The distribution of incomes, even in the richer societies—where starvation may not exist, but injustice is widespread and visible—is so skewed that to shift the balance significantly almost necessarily implies some shifts in political power. The astute statesman can foresee more or less correctly what these shifts are likely to be and may turn the change to his own advantage, like Henry VIII in the sixteenth century who used the dissolution of the monasteries, a long overdue reform, to benefit new classes who would in turn elevate royal power above that of an older federal nobility. In any case, it would be unreasonable to expect that the power initiating the revolutionary change must be entirely altruistic, even though an idealistic motive influences his (or its) final decision. The extraordinary thing about President Johnson's actions in office is that he seemed to start with 'everything made', and with a great opportunity to leave a reforming mark in the cities, and to perpetuate Democratic rule by a programme of successful reform. His failure to do this may unfortunately become a warning to other reformers and a basis for reaction.

It is through politics that the problem of equality within nations is linked with that of inequality between nations. If the national economies of the non-socialist world are categorized into the simple division of the industrialized and rich, and the non-industrialized and poor, it soon becomes apparent that without a substantial shift of capital from one to the other the gap between them must widen not only absolutely but even relatively. This is because the economic link between them, by way of exports and imports, is so structured as to make alienation of the gap, by means of growth in total trade, most unlikely.

The less developed, and largely primary-producing countries, have a high and probably rising propensity to import, since both by emulation in consumption and by need for machinery and capital equipment, they have an unfortunate tendency to want more imports as their incomes grow. The worse the distribution of incomes within the developing countries, the more marked this phenomenon of a high and rising propensity to import will be, for it is the richer segments of these economically backward societies that need and see the advantage of both more consumption and investment goods from abroad.

One remedy for this situation is, on paper, that the rich should be more heavily taxed. But, as already noted, a drastic fiscal reform can hardly be effected unless society as a whole is re-formed, and this implies a social and political upheaval of a fundamental kind, indeed a revolution. Without this political change little can be done in this matter.

Although there is a consensus that some aid should be given by richer to poorer countries, there is little agreement, or implicit consensus even, as to how large the desirable transfers should be. In practice, yet again, political factors impose limitations on the extent of the aid that can be actively given. Whatever United Nations' officials may write in their reports, and whatever resolutions may be passed by meetings of UNCTAD, an organization that deliberately sets out to be a mouthpiece for the developing countries, the political constraints on the amount that each country *can* give (however generous-hearted its government may chance to be) are very real.

Political problems of international giving would arise, if the giving was large enough to be effective,[1] at several levels. The possibility of really large injections of capital into, say, a given primary-producing recipient country would at once raise the question what person, or agency, actually hands out the loan, and in return for what action by the specific recipient? For the making of a gift is itself an act of power. If, as with the 'public law' gifts of wheat to India by the USA, counterpart assets are put into the possession of the official giver (in this case the Congress of the United States) he, or it, will end up with a possibly embarrassing collection of assets (in this case a large share in the total reserves of the Bank of India). If the gifts are made to the government of the recipient country, there may well be 'strings attached'. Critics will, sometimes justly, denounce the transfers as part of a neo-colonial plot. Most French and some Australian aid is given on a strictly neo-colonial basis.

The politics of giving may involve an ultimate giver of last resort. In the long discussion of the international reserves problem, it was assumed often in the 1950s that this giver would be the USA. But in the 1960s, when the USA as well as the UK and other countries, from time to time, were in balance of payments difficulties themselves, the lender or giver of last resort was seen to be Germany. But the West Germans were most reluctant to accept this role, while flattered perhaps to be asked and willing to begin thinking what requests they should put forward for a *quid pro quo* if they ever had to make a major contribution.

The political fact of life is that governments work within constraints imposed by their environment, which is influenced by history as well as current social conditions. On what terms Germany, France or Australia will provide aid to developing

[1] Given the objective of reducing the gap of inequality between nations.

88

countries, which of these countries they will assist and with what proportion of their national incomes, are not exactly predetermined, but they must fall within constraining boundaries. During the so-called development decade of the 1960s, it seemed to become evident that these boundaries would keep the total flow of aid well below the amount needed to close the development gap.

The tendency of the economist, as of the man in the street, is to brush aside 'political constraints', as though these were the whims of fatuous politicians. At best, these constraints are treated as arbitrary external conditions that limit the progress of the (in principle) rational economic forces which yield ever higher standards of living. Perhaps some of this bias may be reduced if consideration is given to how the developing countries might be helped were the constraints totally removed.

If it were likely, for example, that country P, a primary-producing developing country, would in consequence of help from country S, an advanced industrial country, ask to be annexed by country S, and offer, once it had reached a certain standard of living, to contribute taxes and military help to country S, in perpetuity, there would be clear political advantages for country S, in rendering aid to P. Other political advantages might be the provision of convenient bases from which trade routes could be protected, critical waterways guarded, or powerful rivals threatened. These kinds of advantages can be secured by imperialist powers, like France and Britain in the nineteenth century, or the USSR and the USA particularly since World War II. The political advantages of holding certain territories are clear and justify initial or continuing expenditure to secure that they contain viable societies at an adequate living standard. But if help is given 'without strings', in the expectation only of benefits from a stable government, or a better society, in the receiving country— benefits that will be diffused all over the world—the political pay-off for the gift is neither so clear nor so likely.

The giving countries need not be stigmatized as either selfish or imperialistic in wanting some political advantage to accrue from their gifts abroad. Imperialism certainly continues to exist, although apologists for the USA and the USSR continue to deny this obvious fact. But this is a separate issue. If it becomes increasingly possible for the minorities within these imperial systems to assert their identities and to protect their interests through partially democratic institutions, whatever is still oppressive in these systems may eventually be overthrown. What concerns us now is not the existing system, but how to spread wealth to parts of the world not yet wholly within it; how to make it advantageous to the richer nations to help the others without offering to them again any glittering imperial prizes. In a more rational world, where imperialism is no longer tolerated, some alternative way of giving a political advantage to the donor nations is necessary.

Some donors already secure a certain *quid pro quo*. They insist that their gifts be used to employ their own nationals as advisers or administrators, or to finance exports from their own economy, or they go further than this and unofficially use the gifts to pressurize the receiving economy to exclude imports from rival suppliers. Some of these methods of securing an advantage are internationally undesirable, and will in time, it is hoped, be abandoned.

The kind of advantage that might be regarded as more beneficial and lasting is one that has multilateral effects, while at the same time giving a distinct and visible political gain to the donor country. For politicians have to show results and not operate in a situation where the more that is given the greater the unpopularity of the donor. The common impression many highly-taxed American citizens now have is that an ungrateful world uses American dollars to attack American interests overseas. If American aid is to expand, it must surely be at least arguable that the end-result is a more secure world, in which the objectives of American policy are more likely to be achieved and it is not necessarily a reversion to, or an extension of, imperialism to try to put the aid programme on this pragmatic basis.

The alternatives are an appeal either to altruism or to fear.

At some UNCTAD discussions the first of these approaches has been rather persistently used. The basis of the well-known 'Prebisch' position has been that because exporters of primary products tend to secure worse terms of trade than specialists in industrial products—the latter owe, as it were, a donation to the former. They owe it much as the individual rich are normally bound to make gifts to beggars in the street.

There are several objections to this approach, easily the most important being that it is quantitatively ineffective. It is demonstrable within countries that charity is not enough. The glow of righteousness comes to the giver long before the potential recipients have had enough. Hence the welfare states have arisen, in which provision has been made, out of taxation, for the blind, the sick, the aged and other unfortunate groups within the particular community. Within the international community too, charity is never sufficient. Gifts made from charitable motives are not to be regretted or despised, but their total is not likely to meet the objective desired.

If there were a world government, the richer inhabitants of the earth might contribute their taxation directly to an organization that financed developments in the poorer sectors. As things are, the channel still has to be by way of the decisions of so-called sovereign states. For this reason, it is governments—politicians being their spokesmen—that have to be convinced of the advantages of aid.

The motive of fear may sometimes operate successfully. For instance, Australia may feel directly threatened by a social breakdown in Indonesia, the USSR could hardly face the prospect of economic chaos in East Germany, and the United States has traditionally concerned itself with the equilibrium of the major states of South America. But while the motive of fear, combined with that of altruism, may compel advanced countries to take drastic steps to avert famines, or to provide physical resources for countries in desperate situations, these motives are not sufficiently meaningful to support long-hand policies, especially as they operate ambiguously.

If fear of a breakdown in a particular P country really exists, and is based on a likelihood of a serious collapse, the remedy may be to help that country but not to make it strong. Did the United States, or Australia, want to see Indonesia immediately become strong after General Suharto replaced General Soekarno? Surely the interest of the advanced societies dictated caution while the political outcome of the take-over was in doubt. Or does the USSR wish its more unpredictable protégés, in the Middle East or in Eastern Europe, to grow to a scale of strength in which they will have greater initiative and more choice of action? Again, it would seem likely that fear gives a motive for only a carefully controlled aid programme. These are particular instances, but they indicate a quite general rule. One political motive is fear, just as one is a kind of altruism, but neither of these motives imply that a developed country will want to place an undeveloped one so much on its feet that its future actions become unpredictable. Fear of an economic collapse is counter-balanced by fear of an economic miracle.

If the developed countries are to be substantially more motiva-ted than this, conditions will have to arise in which the inter-dependence of political and economic success is more completely realized. Their governments must be able to see political ad-vantages for themselves in the growth of other economies. The necessary condition for generous aid-giving is that the givers should have a strong and continuing motivation, which implies that they must see their political as well as economic fortunes as being partly dependent upon the growth and security of develop-ing countries.

Whether this situation can ever be reached is a matter for speculation and discussion. The point to grasp, with all its implications, is that nothing short of a realization of inter-dependence of interests (if indeed these exist) will adequately motivate politicians to act in ways which will undermine their own power if there is no such interdependence.

If a giving country (an S country) becomes genuinely con-vinced that it has an interest in the improvement of the welfare of P country, it will concern itself not only with transfers of capital to that country but with initiating improvements in its internal structure. Inequality of incomes within the developing country may contribute to a high rate of voluntary saving, but from almost all other points of view extreme inequality is undesirable. From the point of view of a high propensity to import, for example, inequality works in the wrong direction. The greater the inequality the more likely is the propensity to import to be high, imposing a tight restraint on economic growth. Moreover, a very unequal income structure is difficult to reform by moderate means, since the higher income groups will in these circumstances very likely hold the political power.

The giving country, therefore, if it is really concerned to help, often gets involved in the need to promote drastic internal economic reform. The attempt to reduce the inequality between nations leads to a motive to reduce inequality within nations. So far this situation is largely based on description—on 'talk' rather than on action, and only in a few countries have serious reforms been introduced in these circumstances.

The political problem is how to involve an S country so closely with the fortunes of one or more P countries without reviving a new form of the old imperial relationship. The politics of giving has been hidden behind the façade of a set of international institutions. Inevitably, as a kind of crunch is approached in the relationship between the giving and the receiving nations, the interests of the respective parties will have to be examined and realistically spelled out. It is safe to predict that, if the political interests of the giving nations are not better served by gifts in the 1970s than in the 1960s, the total value of transfers, inadequate though they are as pump-primers, will not substantially increase.

CHAPTER 6

ETHICS AND ECONOMICS OF REDISTRIBUTION

There has been a consensus in this century that within advanced countries a reasonable tax system redistributes incomes. Since social welfare principles were explicitly adopted in World War II, with the Beveridge Report in England as a land-mark, the consensus has been extended to an approval of establishing a minimum income for the sick, disabled, aged and unemployed. Less clear, but quite definite, has been the gradual acceptance internationally of the obligation of richer nations to contribute gifts to the developing countries. This became explicit in 1960 at the beginning of the 'decade of development'.

Side by side with ordinary economics, and in a sense apart from it, there has thus developed a theory of gifts. Once it has been agreed that social, and perhaps economic, objectives are best served by a systematic policy of gifts, which is what any form of redistribution implies, the question arises whether any criteria can be found to test the adequacy or efficiency of possible variants of this gift system. The issue may be debated partly in an ethical context, that is in terms of duties, moral obligations and moral purposes, and it may also be regarded, without contradiction, as in itself but one of the many economic issues of today.

For, if there have to be gifts, may not some ways of financing and distributing them contribute more gain, or cause less harm, than others? Is not one underlying motive of a policy of gifts the feeling that without such a policy the economic system, with its blind brutalities, would cease to operate, or would be transformed into a system even more oppressive?

This motive, by the way, may be working in so-called socialist countries as well as within the systems that are mainly capitalist.

94

Inequalities certainly exist in socialist countries, not only of income but of power. Their problems are different in important respects, to the extent, for example, that they have abolished private property and inheritance, but they still need some machinery of economic redistribution. They may be motivated by the fear that repression beyond a certain point would risk more for the system than would some policy of alleviating inequalities.

Wherever gifts are systematically made, there is an implicit admission that the economic system, whatever it is, does not operate well. It is being unjust, or inefficient, or both. If the gift system is well designed, and broadly acceptable, much of the criticism of the system that rests on logical grounds, becomes ineffective.

Gift systems may be seen, then, as means adopted in economic systems for their survival, but they may also be seen from many other points of view.

To identify redistribution with gifts is plausible only for a set of clearly defined political frameworks. The common assumptions in economics are (a) that more equal distribution of incomes and wealth than at present exists is desirable, (b) that this would imply that a majority of relatively poor people must gain from a redistribution programme, while a minority of relatively rich people must lose. This is not the place to discuss the social welfare criteria between which a choice has to be made. These two assumptions are mentioned only to clarify the point that political assumptions are also necessary. For if a redistribution is to be considered desirable and necessary some feasible, or practicable, political action is necessary. The proposed redistribution must, at the very least, not be so distasteful to the taxed classes that they opt out of the society altogether, or devote their power and energies successfully to destroying it from within.

In one or other of the possible democratic set-ups, where the rich content themselves with grumbling against a redistributive tax system, and plotting against it legally—within a framework of law and tolerated political behaviour—they can be said to accept the system. They are in this sense making gifts to the

95

poor through the machinery of the state, since they tacitly support the existence of the state and merely deplore its 'extravagance'.

When the rich no longer take this attitude, but are instead prepared to foment a rebellion, supported partly by foreign aid, against the government, rather than submit to confiscatory taxation, there is a condition of incipient civil war. The state has ceased to exist. There results either a *coup d'état* or a right-wing rebellion, or a drawn-out political stalemate. So long, however, as the classes, from whom wealth or income is to be redistributed, accept the social contract (as eighteenth-century political theory would say) and are prepared to abide by the consequences of elections, they can perhaps be said to be prepared to make gifts to the poor.

Progressive taxation has indeed largely replaced overt charity as a method of relieving hardships, and is accepted willingly by taxpayers as less than the evil of a breakdown of society or of more outrageous demands. On these kinds of political assumptions, taxation and giving may be equated.

While all this is implicit in modern industrial societies, and indeed relegated to the commonplace, the rules are vague and the exact principles unclear. The economists discuss the niceties of the meaning of better off or worse off; they *assume*, in the Cambridge tradition, that greater equality is a morally 'better' form of distribution, but rarely address themselves to reasons for this, or to the extent to which the principle should be applied. The new generation maturing in the 1960s have also found that the principle itself was curiously bloodless. Over the generations, distinguished professors of economics in England, particularly at the older universities, have extolled the merits of equality, without in person attacking either the specific problem, or the highly unequal society in which they have become so well established.

Despite the orthodox economists' lip service to equality, there is little pungent criticism in the literature of the wrongness of inequality. There are occasional sneers at polo-playing, yachts in the Mediterranean or horse-racing, activities which the critics find flippant and unethical partly because they would not enjoy them even to the extent that they have the means of indulging in them. Yet quite poor men might enjoy polo, sailing in good weather or a bet at the course itself—the evidence is overwhelming that millions do. Inequality should not be condemned simply because it allows people to do things that the critics personally regard as extravagant, on the grounds that 'even if we were rich we would not do them'.

There are two threads to the argument for greater equality; first, that inequality is for some reason bad in itself, and ought therefore to be remedied by measures of redistribution; and, secondly, that some optimum degree of inequality will be attended by maximum total output. Possibly, as will be seen, in the last analysis these two threads become quite interwoven, but it is useful to start first by discussing 'dividing up the cake', and secondly, how to make and bake it. The ethical principle is the assumption, that, for dividing up the cake, any departure from equality ought to be justified; the onus of proof is on the one who asserts that an inequality should be observed.

But between whom is the cake divided? Between those who earn by their labour, those who own property (the means of production), those who are too old or sick to work, those without property or work, those who are juvenile and/or in educational institutions, and those who are dependent for any other reason? Equality between the incomes of members of these groups has never been claimed, but we ought to be clear in our minds exactly why not.

There are obvious psychological and practical reasons for not paying an unemployed man or an old age pensioner the same weekly wage as an adult male in employment, but what is the ethical basis of the difference? It would seem that it could be based on one of several grounds. All would surely have to include acceptance of the idea that the principle enjoyed a duty to diminish, but not necessarily to abolish, the inequalities that could result from the free interplay of market forces.

Payments to the less favoured groups in society, not currently in full-time work themselves, would seem to be based more upon the ideal of relieving hardship (and perhaps of establishing some recognized social minimum of life), than upon an abstract of equality itself. The concept of a minimum social payment to needy people has become respectable since the Webbs, and later Beveridge, first systematically defended the idea. It would not be tolerable, in this view, for an advanced society to allow its more unfortunate members in some years to undergo real hardship just because they were old, or young or otherwise economically helpless.

This idea is not of equality, but the idea of the social minimum. Applied within the welfare field, in many places it results in a payment to those with special disadvantages, by reason of old age, sickness or family need of some kind. Sometimes the idea is extended to the younger people, like students at technical colleges and universities, or those undergoing apprenticeship training. All these different groups are essentially regarded as past or future earners by work, who deserve to be supported at a reasonable, but minimum level when other sources of income have failed. They are not allowed to fall below some standard set for 'the poverty line'.

A somewhat different argument is applied to non-earners who are dependent upon earners, or who would be if the familial system had not been disrupted by death, desertion, divorce or disease. In these cases the state as such accepts a measure of responsibility and sometimes even pursues an active policy, as where family allowances are used to encourage large families for population reasons. In general, however, it would seem that the guaranteeing of a minimum income to so-called 'dependents', like children, widows and others who have not necessarily been earners (although some may become so), is placed on a different footing from the transfers to earners out of work, or to the sick or to persons incapacitated by age. These have, in a common view, earned their right to a minimum, or are on their way to doing so while the dependents are a by-product not of the labour market but of the domestic family system. The state steps in, but with an air of substitute patronage, rather than to provide for the rights of active people.

Further, the idea of the social minimum may be extended, as has been done in Australia for many decades, to wage-earners themselves. Legislation then enjoins that no one is employed below some basic minimum wage. This is not so much to support equality between wage-earners, as to guarantee a floor price for industrial labour, so removing the effect that immigrant labour might have in 'securing jobs' and undercutting the existing standards of Australian labour. The idea is to eliminate cut-price labour, and to support the position of the trade unions. Indirectly however, a minimum wage tends to become an equalizing force, and it seems, in the countries where it has operated, to have reduced the dispersion of labour's earnings.

While the goal of equality has remained imprecise and unclear, the principle of reducing inequality in some degree has been widely accepted, if not very severely applied. Even the goal of dividing up the cake more equally has been lost sight of, or pursued only half-heartedly, after the cake has definitely been baked. For example, the enormous earnings and receipts of oil magnates, land developers, shipping and airline operators and multiple-store owners have not been much impaired by progressive taxation. One reason is that beyond a certain figure, the earnings of the rich man tempt him (or his companies) to become international, so that taxation may be substantially avoided. A new race of international personages has appeared, who owe little allegiance to any metropolitan country, and whose lives are peripatetic. Unless some international code for taxing such men is agreed to and implemented, it seems likely that the highly progressive taxation of the advanced countries will result in the adoption of similar patterns of life more widely.

Effective redistribution within national boundaries probably cannot, for this and similar reasons, be pursued much further without international agreements, such as those already operating between different countries in respect of double taxation, and other similar problems. There is at present no suggestion that international measures be taken to equalize incomes; international institutions themselves often pay tax-free salaries.

The second side of redistribution is the effect that it might have on the factors of production. How far will any particular tax system alter the size or distort the pattern of the productive effort made by the income earners? Economists satisfied themselves many years ago that in some circumstances a rise in the incidence of taxation would act as an incentive to additional effort, the general rule being that this would be the effect if the demand for income was sufficiently inelastic. Evidently the converse situation could exist. From time to time researches have tended to show that key decision-takers would often be likely to have an inelastic demand for income and therefore to be favourably effected by taxation rather than the reverse.

It can hardly be pretended that the researches on which this kind of conclusion has been based covered all aspects of the matter, such as the questions of political aspirations, or 'felt' as against 'actual' burdens. To take the latter point first, many taxpayers believe themselves to be paying taxes at quite different rates than they actually are. They feel burdens that are not there, and sometimes overlook burdens that are. To find evidence for these results quantitatively, for a given period, involves expensive opinion research. The important point for the present argument is that redistribution must surely be limited not by the taxes and burdens that an average member of the public actually submits to, but by those to which he thinks he submits. Many British taxpayers in the middle ranges of income believed in 1968 that they were paying far heavier taxes than their West German counterparts, which was the reverse of the truth.[1] Many Australians with middle income ranges mistakenly believed in 1968 that they were more highly taxed than their British opposite numbers.[2] The history of taxation, both before and since the Boston tea

[1] See J. R. Hicks, *Three Banks Review*, 1968.
[2] The newspapers, especially *The Australian*, convinced them of the opposite in 1969.

party, is full of incidents when a relatively trivial change in taxation resulted in a disproportionate political furore.

Once again, and in this context too, international effects and examples may be very important. A high tax on coffee in France may be perfectly supportable there when the number of French visitors to England or the Netherlands is few—and where for the sake of argument we may suppose that there is a low tax on coffee. But once there are two or three million Frenchwomen crossing the frontiers for their holiday, such a *differential* in taxation may become politically insupportable. It may not become necessary for governments to march in step, but it will become progressively harder for them to ignore each other.

Even though no formal suggestions have yet been made how to co-ordinate different national taxation systems, the necessity for doing something of this kind will surely be forced upon governments within the next fifty years. The absence of any movement in this direction is due to several forces, the most obvious being the reluctance of governments to adopt any measures that would dampen the inflow of capital, so long as there is a world shortage of that, and the second major force is no doubt the desire to finance one's own nationals when they are overseas, since whatever they are doing there (except as tourists) they are presumably promoting some form of exports. It would indeed be undesirable from an international point of view, for reasons well established by international trade theory, to place obstacles to the flow of capital from one country to another, unless there was some clear social-welfare gain to be won by a measure which, on first principles, must be harmful to growth. Nevertheless, from the point of view of distributive justice, it is difficult to see how even such progressive taxes as are now in existence (and they are affecting overall distribution in the long term only gradually) can be effective so long as tax havens exist and international travel becomes faster and easier. It was written into the Rome Treaty not only that there should be a free movement of capital (and of labour) within the European Community, but also that eventually national fiscal measures should be co-ordinated. If the Community could move forward on this point, it would indeed be setting an example to the world.

Difficulties of agreement include the fact that national traditions are sometimes strong and well-supported intellectually. For instance, the Italian economists have made notable contributions to the theory of public finance. They have tended to favour proportional rather than progressive taxation, and to be sceptical of social and governmental activities. Their special definition of national income reflects an anxiety that savings should not be taxed, and that the dynamism of capitalists should be encouraged.

The fundamental ethics of a gift system could be based on four possible principles. The first, similar to the precept of charity, would be that any person, A, blessed with more resources than his neighbour B, should give B enough to equalize their net receipts. This may be in accordance with some views of justice or equality, but it is not much practised, and is not in consonance with most modern views of fair play, nor with economic theorizing about incentives, so it need not be further discussed. The second is that gifts should be made whenever B is in dire straits, threatened by starvation or in some way liable to extreme personal disaster if help is not forthcoming. Members of many societies recognize an obligation in such cases, and it is not questioned that gifts should be made for rescue purposes, but this second principle is inadequate as a basis for long-term equalizing action.

A third principle would be that gifts should be made because rather less unequal conditions than would otherwise prevail was a 'better' state of affairs morally. This is probably the principle implied by many of our actions today, both within and between nations. What has not been thought out is the possibility of a fourth principle, not so extreme as the first, but more drastic than the third. The fourth possible principle would assert that gifts should be made so as to cause actual net losses to the givers (make them noticeably less well-off) and to provide substantial gains for the receivers, and the principle would imply that 'equalization' must be given the meaning that the dispersion of net incomes (or wealth) was substantially improved by the system. This fourth principle has not, so far as can be ascertained, ever been implemented. Perhaps the current unrest in society is partly bound up with a demand for 'real justice' that implies some recognition of this principle.

What would be the economics of a system of redistribution based on this principle? What would its political foundation really be? In other words, can circumstances be imagined in which it became practicable to operate such a system at all? These questions can be answered only speculatively since there is little empirical evidence of how such systems would come into being or be worked.

The economics of redistribution are deeply interwoven with the politics, since both operate through the effects on individuals' motivation of any social action, such as the imposition of taxes. To illustrate, a group of individuals in a clearly defined 'nation' will respond to a campaign to bear sacrifices to attain a national goal in quite a different way than another group, perhaps just as large and just as well-off, without this national spirit. Despite this close connexion, it is possible to isolate the economic aspect of redistribution, and to consider what types of economic, as distinct from political goals, a society may be able to choose between—in general, what its economic options really are.

The economic purpose of redistribution may be presumed to be to put the members of the society in the most preferred position available to them. This must take into account the values (which of course may be changing) currently prevalent in the society. Redistribution must in some sense of this kind make our society better off, after all its repercussions have been taken into account.

What we have to imagine is an attempt to change seriously and significantly the dispersion of real incomes, after tax costs and social benefits from government expenditure have all been imputed correctly. This is a different matter from reckoning, at first blow, the dispersion of pre-tax incomes. One promising line of enquiry would be to see what additional services could be provided, either through the market system or through publicly financial activities, with the object of improving human efficiency in production. This process is nowadays often referred to as 'investing in human capital'. This concept in itself cuts across the Keynesian division of output into C (consumption goods) and I (investment goods), since it becomes clear that, in a significant sense, part of C may be regarded as part of total social investment. The additional services to be provided might be in the fields of formal education, expansion of 'popular' education (not propaganda, but a high quality of material disseminated through mass media), mass transport of people on vacations to national or international 'shrines', meeting-halls, museums and places of interest, part-time educational courses at all levels, and so on. There is already activity in all these fields. The pressing need to raise the productivity of the human worker suggests however, that in no country would additional provision of such services be redundant. The only question is how to provide them, and the best answer has to be found to meet varying local circumstances.

The outcry for 'participation', and the student turbulence in schools and universities, is in part a reflection of the inadequacy and failure of formal educational procedures. This is not just a question of gimmicks or teaching devices, like the introduction of learning programmes. Education consists of a stimulus being given to students, so that their energies may be directed towards constructive self-development. They may genuinely need more discussions, more chances to try out their own—often badly formed—ideas, more chances to explain what they find difficult, and more opportunities to express their doubts and anxieties. But all this, even if provided, will not add up to education unless the students can work and educate themselves.

A true lasting basis for reducing the dispersion of incomes in society can only be a just law on inheritance, and a maximum of educational opportunity for people of all ages (at least up till fifty), but there will still be needed the mechanism for organizing the new, more contentious and better-educated society. There will still be needed a modern system of industrial relations, codes of conduct for the relationship between employers and employed, as well as a legal system that operates effectively and impartially. Only within an improved social and political framework can incomes be determined satisfactorily.

In international affairs, the third principle of giving is usually invoked. Recognition is widespread that relief of emergencies (as enjoined by the second principle) is not enough. The third principle goes further than this, but it is still not much more demanding than the malaise in conscience which underlay the private charities of Dickensian England. Many countries, particularly Australia in recent years, can temper the embarrassment of their middling classes at the rising material standards by flag days and public appeals for funds. The most successful of these appeals are those like the 'Heart Campaign' that rely on fear or self-interest rather than those for 'boys' homes' or 'Aboriginal advancement' which are subjects of less direct interest to donors.

To go beyond the third principle to the fourth would seem therefore to be impractical. The demands that its implementation would make would be more serious. Instead of relatively harmless charity, actual self-sacrifice would be required. It would indeed be quixotic to expect any such change of principles unless some change in circumstances occurs that makes its adoption necessary.

The third principle, the charity principle, is at present the basis of inter-governmental as well as private charity. The idea often seems to be to give substantially, but not even as much as 1 per cent of national income in total, through government channels, and to encourage private charities to add another fraction of 1 per cent to this total. The gifts provide some slight benefits to the receivers, but their main function seems to be to relieve the guilt feelings of the donors, and to enable them, at governmental level, to hold up their heads at international conferences.

The whole gift system, elaborate as it is, that operates under the third principle, is based on the belief that it is morally good for the better-off countries to give to the poorer, with an unexpressed corollary that the amount of the gift is not of much importance. So long as the gifts flow, the twinges of guilt are assuaged and also a reasonably grateful stance will be adopted by recipients. However, there seems to be nothing in this system of international morality that stipulates that the gifts should be of such a magnitude as fundamentally to change the relative economic situation of giver and receiver. All that matters, is that the rich should not fail in their duty, which consists in handing over some part of their current surplus which they can spare without a serious inconvenience. These strictures apply as much to the USSR as to other major countries, except that some of the Soviet loans are more generously priced than the capitalist ones, whether owing to some doctrinaire miscalculation or to genuine simple generosity, it is hard to say.

The fourth principle is not likely to be invoked as a basis for action unless the richer countries, or their leaders, begin to believe that the gifts they must make should be made in their own interest, and that these gifts should be substantial. No group of individuals, nor a nation, is likely to give to the point of actual sacrifice, except in the belief that this is necessary for self-preservation.

The sad fact is that the plight of the new industrial masses led to little in the way of sanitary legislation for the growing cities and towns of the industrial revolution, until their condition (with cholera and other epidemics) threatened the survival of the better-off citizens. So, in the twentieth century the most likely force to galvanize the rich into drastic action will be the fear of disease, unrest and subversion spreading from the poor and over-populated regions into the comparatively well-ordered parts of the globe. Under a clear threat, but only under that, governments will be willing to try to persuade their electorates that a sacrifice is needed.

This situation may or may not arise. It is possible that solutions will be found to the world's population and growth problems without threats of this kind ever materializing. All that can be said is that experts of many kinds find such a future to be most unlikely. The population explosion, the manpower problem, and the recurrent crises in international confidence in monetary arrangements, all make the belief that there is a simple, uninterrupted progression to a better life somewhat unacceptable.

The point of the argument is, however, not whether the fourth principle is ever going, in practice, to be applied, but whether it is right or wrong. Some would answer that this depended upon circumstances. Suppose that the facts were these: relative poverty in the developing nations can *never* be relieved on a permanent basis, without a build-up period, so expensive that outside help must be at least large enough to set back the last-resort donors. In this case, perhaps there is a moral obligation to give. If, on the other hand, poverty *could* be successfully alleviated more slowly, the large gifts would neither be of such importance nor so likely to be made.

If people are living at a level of, say, $150 per head a year in a poor country, and at $3,200 a year in a rich one, is there some moral obligation on the richer one to reduce its income to, say, $3,100 in order to raise the income of the poor country by $100 a head? (The assumptions are that the problem of transferring income can be overcome and that the population of the poor country is, and remains at, double that of the rich one.) And if to $3,100 why not to $3,000? This issue seems never to be discussed.

In this age of benefit cost studies, and attempts to rationalize the priorities of the Pentagon's expenditures, which involves putting a price on human lives and a valuation upon a victorious military skirmish, there is nothing especially far-fetched or ridiculous in trying to quantify the benefits of a particular gift. How much is it worth to the giving country, A, to see the receiving country, B, expand its national income by 50 per cent? There must be some gain, moral or political, or some addition to the security of the giver, or the policy would not be under serious discussion. Most international gifts since 1947 have had some fairly crude and obvious motivation, and although it is to be hoped that, as conditions in the world improve, the gains will

be more general and accrue to wider sections of humanity, some
similar calculations will remain.

An acceptable moral principle might be that gifts should be
made for the political advantage of the giver, but only if the
gifts were in total so large as to cause the giver some genuine
difficulties in making them. Britain has sometimes been criticized
for its comparatively open-door policy to persons of different
nationalities and races, a policy that had to be modified under
internal pressures; but surely the way to look at this episode was,
first, to note that there were considerable economic advantages to
British people from the policy itself (labour supply being short),
and secondly that such political and social inconveniences as the
policy occasioned were evidence of a generous approach that
risked some costs in order to uphold a humane principle. Action
was needed not to reverse the policy but to ameliorate its less
pleasant consequences.

The principle of giving till it hurts is not an easy one to
advocate. But most of the advanced and prosperous peoples are
living in a lull between two periods of international organization.
The first was the period of the nineteenth-century empires. The
second cannot be foreshadowed, but must necessarily arise from
the built-in conflict of interests between the future haves and
have-nots. Which side will realize first the absolute necessity of
a new deal? Possibly the have-nots, under the leadership of men
like Prebisch, or prophets like Myrdal. But the first action may
result not from their claims. More likely the great trading and
financial interests of the world will be impelled to take action so as
to ensure growing markets, and an orderly growth in economic
organization. The great international companies will not be
able to forgo international trade, or entry into the new nationalistic economies. They will press the international organizations
(like the World Bank and the UN department of economic and
social affairs) to underpin the social capital of the developing
countries. They will ask their own governments to take measures
to encourage development in other countries as well as their own.

Enormous disasters could overcome the peaceful trade of the

world if international growth does not attain an accelerated momentum. The economies of scale that result from jumbo jets, giant oil tankers, massive banks of data-processing machinery and all the rest of the modern paraphernalia depend upon larger markets and rising purchasing power in the hands of the industrial masses everywhere. In this future world the argument of preservation and self-interest may be stronger than it is today, and it may constrain the future propagandists and decision makers to demand gifts that will be like Rockefeller donations instead of sixpences in a flag-day box.

CHAPTER 7

INEQUALITY AND DEVELOPING ECONOMIES

Within Economies

The inequality of incomes and wealth inside the developing countries is often very high, and almost always much more extreme than within the moderately prosperous economies. The very richest groups of countries like the USA and its near imitators, have, it is true, extremes of wealth and income, often imperfectly measured by the official statistics. But they also have considerable social and economic mobility; they have adopted traditions and policies that promote relatively easy movement up the social ladder, and from one employment to another, and, in the case of the US especially there is a traditional belief in equality of opportunity that offsets some of the consequences of the other tradition of respect for money.

Concern with the inequalities prevailing in the poorer countries is based on both social and economic considerations. Societies with great extremes of wealth are difficult to organize, and always liable to be seriously damaged, if not entirely disrupted, by sporadic outbursts of discontent from the less than highest ranks of society.

The main economic dangers of gross inequalities are simply that they work directly against some of the moral objectives of an economic society. Inequalities may be first a danger to productive efficiency. To allocate resources to the most suitable uses is one of the tasks to be performed, and in a very unequal system the rewards for the factors of production may not remain appropriate for this task. Secondly, the supply of savings may depend upon an unequal distribution of incomes, and indeed for this reason many eminent theorists used to advocate more, not less, inequality in the early years of development.

Sociologists, and other critics of the development process, as it has actually worked out in the 1950s and 1960s, are often inclined to argue that, in the long run, one of the factors necessary for development is in fact egalitarianism.[1] Unless the actual distribution of real goods produced is not carried out on a 'performance oriented' basis—that is, unless goods are offered in proportion to the social value of the performance of the worker (in any work role)—the economy can hardly begin to develop. This leads towards egalitarian ideas, although it may stop short of the successful introduction of a new ideology. At least, the tendency to spread earnings around is very strong. Part of any new equality will depend upon government-sponsored schemes. The developing countries thus engage themselves in the politics of equality. They all have learnt something about welfare schemes, and they have their own views on distributive justice. Under this pressure the governments tend to play a waiting game but, whether willingly or not, they are drawn into a political battle, the battle of equality, which is one of the most confused struggles of all.

In the twilight zone between politics, sociology, history and economics, it is difficult to see clearly, or to know which filter to put on the torchlight of one's own reasoning powers. But there are some recognizable features of the struggle for equality, which so often is a subordinate theme of the struggle for development. Often the armed forces, or just the army, emerges as a dynamic operator. The army in a developing country with an obsolescent, hierarchical social structure may be a levelling influence. It may be relatively incorrupt, and offer the only reliable semi-permanent social system with loyalties a little more than opportunist. This may be in strong contrast to existing political parties, or élites that have become hereditary,

[1] See *A Reappraisal of Economic Development* edited by Andrew H. Whiteford (Chicago, 1967). See also G. Myrdal, *Asian Drama* (London: Allen Lamb, 1968), p. 747 '... it is possible to point to a number of conditions that suggest that [in India] ... an increase in equality would help rather than hinder development ...'.

indolent and ineffective. But while armies provide ladders for social advancement, and sometimes a machinery for social services of a kind (particularly for families of the forces' members) they rarely provide leaders capable of adequate civilian social reforms. The kind of greater equality that results from welfare legislation can only, it seems, be promoted by civilian leaders of great vision and character.

Overt egalitarian policies are, then, likely to be the consequence rather than the cause of economic development. If they had come first they probably would have helped that development to begin, or to flourish, and where social legislation has come fairly early, as in India in education and some aspects of health planning, the contribution has been by no means negligible.

But unfortunately, social legislation is probably not a necessary condition for early economic growth, and the first step towards development may be taken without much regard for social costs. A time may come when neglect of social costs results in some very expensive but predictable social evils that can only be overcome by large-scale campaigns. For example, a criminal thieving class may be created, whose way of life is organized around burgling or pilfering. The later costs of containing the activities of this new class, so that incomes and wealth are not seriously threatened, may be extremely high, but nevertheless it is hard to change the earlier attitudes to these problems.

Economic inequality within nations is difficult to measure consistently, both because of poor data and of the difficulties of international comparisons at these levels of incomes. One way of indicating the dispersion of incomes is to compare the average with the median income of a country. An average very much higher than the median indicates a relative bunching of the higher incomes towards the top of the scale. In advanced countries, like Australia and New Zealand, the excess of the average over the median incomes is only 13 or 14 per cent (although it has been lower in Australia, it is now tending to increase). In countries like Ceylon, India and Pakistan it may run as high as from 30 to 50 per cent.[1] The difficulty in obtaining comparable readings of this statistic is that distribution of income figures are often compiled from a different base, with a varying proportion of total income earners omitted at the lower end as exempted from tax or not receiving any significant income.

In developing countries the distribution of incomes among income earners is closely linked with their distribution among major classes of occupation. In general, incomes earned in agriculture are much lower than those earned in the cities in various forms of industry. A country with a high percentage of rural workers tends, therefore, to be biased towards an appearance of greater inequality. On the other hand, *within* the agricultural sector incomes are distributed in a more egalitarian fashion usually than in industry, so that this partly compensates for the difference between the two kinds of major activity.

Another 'functional' way of dividing up a nation's receipts is between:

(a) wage and salary earners
(b) self-employed and entrepreneurs
(c) asset owners.

Assets usually amount to somewhere between four and six times the national income. The self-employed and entrepreneurs usually own some of the assets (from 75 per cent of the total downwards), so they receive two classes of income, one from their property and another from their current activities. The rate of yield on assets may vary usually from 6 to 12 per cent over the long run. As these values have all fluctuated, trends in the shares of asset-owners, workers, etc., are all hard to discern. In some 'advanced' countries the share of income due to assets declined between two world wars, but in others (like France and the USA) very little decline was observed.

In recent decades, the share of groups (a) has tended to rise as a long-run trend. Employees became a more important section of the total labour force, partly because investments had

[1] See figures produced by Colin Clark in 1957.

raised the output of labour, by better machines and by education. An increasingly high priority, so it has been said, is being given to the quality of labour used. In some countries, particularly the United Kingdom, there was stability in the share of the national income taken by wages for fairly long periods. But generally the many improvements in techniques, in organization, in scale of operation, in specialization and in human effectiveness as the number of hours worked per week declined, have all been reflected in rising employee incomes per head, and employees have become a more important element in the labour force as a whole since the late nineteenth century. Techniques and possibilities for development are changing, so it cannot be assumed without detailed examination that the pattern of advance of the industrialized countries will be repeated by the poorer developing countries of today. Nevertheless, the historical experience of the 'advanced' Western economies suggests that development could well mean the creation in the developing economies of a broadly-based labour force with increasing earning power.

Examination of the manpower needs of the developing countries confirms the economic need for the enlargement of the skilled labour force. Typically they have a surplus of untrained, and a severe shortage of trained, personnel—almost regardless of where the cut-off line between 'trained' and 'untrained' is drawn. There is a shortage in most developing countries not only of doctors, professors, engineers and executives, but of foremen, craftsmen, machine-workers and book-keepers. The creation of whole new cadres of workers in the semi-skilled, skilled and highly skilled categories will only be possible if incomes can be distributed in an appropriate way, which implies a reduction in the extreme polarization of wealth. At least in the medium term this implies some equalization of incomes, as well as a rise in average income.

All this is widely believed—at least in circles of international do-gooders. To a limited extent, too, the commonplace here is probably true. What the International Labour Office propounds year after year through its well-staffed organization, its literature and its conferences, is precisely that training, manpower planning, employment organization and other programmes will assist developing countries not only to attain higher average incomes, but to acquire a more liberal social structure. They are invited to learn from, and to some extent model their economies on, the advanced economies, which, it is implied, are well 'ahead' of them not only in wealth and income, but in social security arrangements, progressive taxation, honest government and even equality of opportunity.

It is well to remember the kind of doubts that such writers as Titmuss and Galbraith, and the political analysis of power, are able to throw on the validity of the image that Western industrial society likes to build up for itself. To begin with, the statistics collected by capitalist governments are grossly biased, if not as much as, at least in a disturbingly comparable degree with, statistics of the so-called socialist countries. The really important facts as to distribution of wealth and income between individuals are hidden because of laws on company formation or rules of secrecy. If this is so, are the 'advanced' countries really setting so good an example as is commonly taken for granted?

On the surface, no doubt, there is greater fairness and justice in countries with well-organized tax systems, where the principle of progressive taxation has long been implemented, than in countries which still have to rely on regressive indirect taxes, especially since the richer, well-administered countries can and do provide much more extensive social services than the backward countries. But this tends to overlook the possible dynamic forces constantly at work in the two types of economy. The process of accumulation, with all its consequences, is going on in both. The tendency for the powerful and the rich to become more powerful and richer may be even stronger in the advanced than in the less-developed economies; as was noted in Chapter 4 above, there are economic forces of great power in conflict in this area. Statistics are lacking to show truthfully what is happening—whether or not the polarization of wealth and income into the hands of small groups is offsetting the concessions to the masses which is forced out of the world's decision-makers.

In the developing countries the rulers should perhaps pay less attention to the analogies of other, and quite different, societies than to their own special problems. They, too, may need to hit on some level of inequalities that is widely acceptable in their own place and time, and dynamically they must ensure also that the rate of change not only in the average income but in its dispersion is conformable with the popular will.

This is a hard lesson for the new regimes of the 'third world' to learn, and an even harder one to practise, or put into effect. Much of the third world came into existence politically on the wave of anti-imperialism and de-colonization that swept most of the older European empires in the 1950s. No one wants to restore those empires, or to overlook their fatal flaw—a moral one—or defend the absurdities of the ideologies (partly racial) on which they were based. Nevertheless, it was a pity, for the sake of the third world itself, that their own propaganda went so far as to deny the realities of the earlier situation. They, the old empires, were not exclusively exploitative, as is so often pretended, nor were they devoid of social value. Myrdal finds himself unable to explain the existence of a flourishing textile industry in India in 1914, and an established iron and steel industry, since these phenomena were counter to his supposition that the British raj opposed all industrial development. He justifies the existence of a money-lending class *after* independence, as the only socially possible way of wringing some of the economic surplus from the peasants, but of course condemns the same system while foreign rule prevailed.

The exaggerations of the evils of imperialism are really un-necessary since there are plenty of valid objections to such a system. But worse than that, to diagnose wrongly the evils of society leads to incorrect or wildly impracticable politics. Gandhi, and to some extent Nehru, seemed seriously to believe that once the British rule had been removed the forces of democratic liberty in India would well-up and establish complete equality. Not only would economic equality be demanded by the irresistible voice of the people; the caste system would disappear, and the rich and privileged members of society would voluntarily give up their privileges.

All these delusions have now been exposed or forgotten. They arose from earlier errors, and from a factually incorrect description of the then existing social system.

Fortunately, the element of idealism, which was the saving feature of the Indian ideals of socialism and equality, has not entirely disappeared. In India and in other developing countries there remain leaders and intellectuals who have been hardened by the disappointments of the early years of planning and development—whether experienced by themselves or their predecessors if they are young—and who now look realistically to a long haul before establishing more equal conditions.

The factors that are favourable to greater equality have been skilfully identified by Myrdal. He points out that greater social equality is almost essential to greater productivity. Everything that the caste system stands for is hostile to productivity. Malnutrition and poor health and low consumption of essential protective foodstuffs work against productivity, and greater economic equality must therefore improve the chances of raising real output per head.

Myrdal judiciously thinks that the rich can be divided into two groups, those who indulge in greater wasteful conspicuous consumption as they become richer, and those who make (as entrepreneurs) greater use of their gains in a productive manner. The division of the rich into these two classes is reminiscent of the debates on the subject between Malthus and Ricardo, and Adam Smith's comments. The question is probably not so simple to resolve. The 'wasteful' (and indeed even aesthetically or morally disgusting) expenditure of some rich people may, or may not, be 'economically' desirable, in the sense of tending to maximize total national income, depending on its employment-multiplier effects and the particular conjuncture facing the economy. The money pouring into the hands of the entrepreneur may or may not be of great national economic worth depending upon the wisdom (or national relevance) of the decisions that he makes on its expenditure.

While there is no easy recipe, the possibility exists that a society can develop with greater equality rather than less achieved at each stage of its advance. To follow this path may in fact be difficult, but it is comforting to know that at least the objective can be gained this way.

There is a danger that, on the contrary, there will be a failure to achieve any equalization at all. If so, the record of the governments in the developing countries will be so much in conflict with their professed intentions, that eventually instability of the regimes will become chronic. Something of this sort has occurred in Latin America.

The developing countries, like the developed, have to face a dynamic and not a static economic problem. They do not simply have to engineer a once for all equalization of incomes and of wealth. The problem for them is to find a way of changing incomes and wealth as their economies develop in an equalizing rather than a dispersing manner. They too have to decide on an incomes policy, and one which works consistently with their developmental objectives.

Between Economies

At this point the 'within countries' problems link up with 'between countries' problems. The inequalities that will be acceptable within a particular country, at a given date, are likely to be dependent upon the systems adopted in other countries, and also on the different average levels of income and wealth in them. For instance, it would hardly be possible for Indonesian income distribution to be wholly unaffected by changes in Malaysia, or Pakistani distribution not to be influenced by Indian. If, too, a neighbouring country, with similar natural resources, maintains a persistently much higher income per head than a developing country, this must tend to lead to criticism of that country's public and private leaders.

The reactions within the developing country need not be—

and almost always are not likely to be—wholly rational and calculating. The usual inference made widely in the poorer of two neighbouring countries is that the richer one has gained its advantage by some unfair or underhand practices, and only at levels of sophisticated discourse, among educated minorities, are alternative explanations sought. However, with improved mass communications, and perhaps with some control of parochial and charismatic press owners, a rational view may become widely accepted.

If so, then a balance can be struck; the distributions appropriate to the two regimes may be received without violent opposition, and even if they differ from each other they may survive symbiotically in a kind of harmony.

If the differences between countries are wide enough, however, the problems of capital movements, and of aid, and of freer exchanges of goods and services have to be solved. So too, has the problem of desired migration. For, whatever the shortcomings of migration as a means of solving serious population growth problems, migration remains, and will remain, a problem in its own right. As long as there are people willing to migrate in large numbers to improve their economic condition, there will be pressure on the better-off countries to assimilate them.

Thus in addition to the ethical and political issues involved in deciding how much international aid should flow between rich and poor countries, there are problems of internal distribution of incomes, and of the many economic relationships between countries that affect the inequalities of both kinds that are tolerable. The unfortunate fact is that while much of the world is entering on a period of unprecedented discovery and economic growth, based on an advancing technology too complex in its ramifications for anyone to grasp or summarize, the rest of mankind is facing a possibly severe and prolonged decline or stagnation in living standards. So harsh a contrast is not really likely to be tolerated for decades, and some answer has to be found.

To avoid the naïveties of the idealists in India who looked for a day when the rich and powerful would voluntarily relinquish their privileges, and to avoid the equally naïve ramblings of the new revolutionists who believe that modern economies can be more justly run by a series of village meetings (and participatory denouncing) is not easy. A political device is needed which maintains communications and genuine popular support without being either childish or the child of doctrinaire oratorical prolixity. It must be effective, acceptable and not taken from a dream.

If the political device can be found—it is likely only to evolve from some streamlined version of an existing institution—there still remains the task for it of implementing a policy.

That policy, as it can now be seen, would have to be very thorough within countries and between countries. The huge acts of charity that are needed between nations can never take place within our existing political and social frameworks, nor will they take place unless the disparities of incomes at home are made acceptable. Just as, in the extreme example of the United States, the Vietnam war and the international aid programmes could not be sustained at mounting cost—despite the mounting total national income—without a serious protest movement being stirred into activity, so the future needs of the developing world, which will quantitatively be much greater than anything so far experienced (for population reasons and others), will not be met unless the giving countries can put their own houses in order. It is, moreover, almost as difficult to receive as to give. The developing countries need internal reform and flexible policies, to be able to receive and to digest the massive gifts that they ought to get.

Even the most elementary relief programmes have often failed, or been hampered, because of an absence of an efficient distributive system. If a society cannot distribute its increasing real income to most of its members, it will remain economically and socially backward.

To obtain the necessary motivation, and to get up the head of steam needed to drive these changes through, each of mankind generally has to be convinced that his own survival and future depends on his neighbour's standard of life. There is no longer anything to be gained, on the world canvas, by having poor neighbours, as the risk to ourselves is too great. It is true that risks are also involved in a raising of standards. Some communities will behave, when they are better off, in ways that will greatly annoy, disturb or even threaten some of the better-off countries and individual families. But these risks are surely likely to be less than the much greater risk of collapse of societies if acceptable material prosperity is not shared out. It is not possible to believe that economic growth, and higher incomes, will suffice to remove the tribal jealousies and aggressions that groups of people entertain for each other, but it is possible to believe that without economic growth, and a tolerable spread of its benefits, these jealousies and aggressions will become more morbid and dangerous.

With economic growth it is just possible that the wars and disturbances that will still occur may become manageable in the sense that they can be isolated and neutralized by swift international action, as a few international incidents already have been. But above all men must feel that it is true that their own interests are bound up with sound government and reasonably just forms of economic distribution within and between all the major peoples of the world.

CHAPTER 8

INCOME DETERMINATION

How net incomes are determined in modern industrial societies is not easy to discover or even to describe. Even the end-result, the actual distribution of incomes after tax, can be analysed only in broad terms. The process of determination includes several stages of adjustment and bargaining. There are the market factors, the supply of and demand for certain specific skills and abilities. There is the whole bargaining set-up, for individuals and groups, the professional societies, the trade unions, and the shop stewards, the arbitration procedures, the employers' federations, the legislated arbitration machinery, and the tax system all affect the final outcome. The way that this whole complex machine is operated may also change from year to year.

The incidence of strikes and industrial stoppages is not only the symptom of the intensity of the struggles that go on between different groups before net incomes are decided, but it has some value as an indicator of conflict. The rise in this incidence in some countries in recent years seems to reflect a general malaise.

Two main factors have effected this. First, there is a growing resistance to redistribution itself. On the one hand, governments have to promise to remedy the consequences of inequality, and to secure the national independence of their country. For the first of these purposes, they must raise and spend increasing sums on health, education and pensions of various kinds, and for the second they must provide considerable sums for defence. These commitments, if taxes are rather inelastic, create a definite pressure towards inflation. But if inflation occurs, that is if prices in general rise from year to year, the demands for increased wages and salaries become more frequent and insistent. No group wants to become the one that contributes most to redistribution by lagging behind in the various series of 'rounds' of wage and salary increases.

Apart from a few exceptional years, these forces have been strong enough to force up wages and prices year after year, despite the fact that the physical output of goods has also been rising. Modern industrial society has developed a tendency towards built-in inflation. This must surely be largely due to the struggle between groups for a share in the total national income. Each group accepts (by its voting behaviour) the idea of re-distributing 'the cake', but also, in its negotiating capacity, refuses to contribute too much to that redistribution.

The second factor in the malaise is that people are better off. This seems to result in two changes. They are now better equipped with savings, and current expenditure is underwritten by social services. More can afford the luxury of strike action. Moreover, as real incomes rise, the rewards of being ahead in the queue of claimants for rises in the pay packet become more substantial.

The various 'rounds' of increases go faster and faster until they result in a political crisis. Governments trying to fight off inflation at home, or destruction of their currencies, use delaying tactics as long as they can. Faced with this situation, governments of the European economies have tried to evolve 'income policies' designed to relate wage agreements to the external economic balance of the country. A similar purpose was introduced into the Australian arbitration system in the early 1960s.

Income policies then became the battleground of the struggle between the classes, if that is a correct term. More accurately the determination of earned incomes alone was brought under this heading. This left out of account the incomes going to owners of land and of capital as rent profits and interest.

Inflation has anti-egalitarian tendencies in at least three ways, by penalizing fixed-income receivers (which includes pensioners), by bringing into the taxation bracket income receivers who were previously wholly or largely exempt from taxation—a very regressive effect—and by promoting high rents and profits.

Whenever the net effect of the three-cornered struggle between employers, employed and government agencies is to permit another round of inflation of prices, all these anti-egalitarian results arise. The employers and the employed in any particular industry may not be particularly worried by this fact. They can, as it were, buy time at the expense of the community at large. The inflation, however, both thwarts the previous intentions of the government to equalize after-tax incomes, and also threatens the balance of payments or the stability of the exchanges. This diminishes the capacity of the country to contribute further to international gifts and loans.

This well-known vicious circle has become the characteristic dilemma of many economies, either openly or at least as a constant danger. The curious fact is that the inflationary danger has become worse as real incomes have risen. It is as though the energy that each group puts into maintaining its place in the pecking order has become greater, the higher the absolute standard of living of its members. The shift to rents and profits has contributed to the intransigence of workers; and the rise in capital values accruing to property owners, even though taxed, has made it difficult for arbitrators, or government-appointed committees investigating wage claims, to resist demands for higher wages.

Inflation, it may be thought, is a lesser evil than deflation. While this may be true, the situation remains that beyond some point the struggle between industrial groups to increase their shares of total national income may result in a decrease in the income to be shared. This will occur when the loss of real income due to the disincentive effects of more regressive taxes, the loss of production due to strikes or go-slow campaigns, and the effects of the sabotage of key industries by political militants become really substantial. Inflation may be due in a sense to the ambition of successive groups of claimants to secure their 'fair share' of the rising national income, but, in the ways described, inflation may lead to a far less equal distribution of incomes throughout the economy.

If this is a fair description of the struggle over distribution currently taking place in many 'advanced' Western economies, in the less developed economies the same forces are at work, sometimes more nakedly. The inflations that occur are more extreme. Instead of negotiations there may be riots.

That economic policy has had to be built, in many countries, around the problem of incomes policy is surely not accidental, but the consequence of the central importance of income distribution. Even more important for growth may be the rate of technological change, and the formation of capital. Income distribution however must be 'settled' (and resettled) continuously with some degreee of success, or the economy will stagger from crisis to crisis.

For this reason, sooner or later, by discussion, by revolution, or by consensus, any economy has to adopt a norm, a code of behaviour which it tries to uphold, and which can be maintained with reasonable success. The thesis so often advanced in the past has been that the ideal should be equality. R. H. Tawney eloquently advocated this, and derided as unnecessary and unjust the inequalities of established British society of the first half of the twentieth century. Much experience of many economies has been collated since he wrote. No one denies that many of the inequalities, even in present society, are probably indefensibly and economically unnecessary. But the theme of this study is that some inequality is necessary, and that a consensus ought to be possible as to the acceptable range and purpose of necessary inequalities. Unless this is possible, it is difficult to see where the struggle for so-called fair shares will lead, other than to a break-down of the societies by a process of escalation in industrial conflict.

The present vogue for protest marches, picketing and non-cooperation arises partly from deep and widespread dissatisfaction with the social order. It is not suggested that this dissatisfaction is wholly irrational or unjustified. But it seems likely that the successive waves of indignation worked up over wage claims are somewhat factitious and could be reduced without the dynamic basis for reform being lost. The need for inequality should be recognized, and the struggles should be over, first, what degree of inequality a given economy should accept (what should the range and scales of rewards become), and, secondly, to what level on the scale should any particular post be related.

The determination of incomes is never likely to be a simple matter, or at least that must be the view of those who believe that social arrangements are complex. It would be simplifying the issue unduly to regard the present struggle over incomes as a clash between two classes, owners and employed, on classical Marxist lines. Some elements in the present situation admittedly give support to this simplification. There is at last taking place that trend to monopolization of ownership by a few which Marx thought would take place, and there is consequent polarization of interests. But on the other hand the 'immiseration' of the workers has not been widespread, and the struggle over incomes is less an attack by workers on owners than a series of attempts of each group of workers to maintain its position on an existing scale.

The apostles of Marxist conflict have tried to teach us that conflict has a valuable function within social systems. This may sometimes be true, and is acceptable so long as it is recognized that open conflict may be destructive, and retrogressive as well— confrontation may be either stimulating or the reverse. Some gains came out of the Thirty Years War, for example, but the general opinion seems to be correct, that on balance that series of conflicts resulted in stagnation in Germany that could have been avoided. The mystical view of Sorel, that violence restores energy to both sides in a struggle, seems to be dubious as a universal generalization.

What is deplorable is not only mounting violence in the struggle over the determination of incomes as such, but the relatively pointless results in relation to the costs incurred. After immense effort, little has been done to improve the distribution of incomes in either an egalitarian direction or towards a pattern that could be justified.

What society needs is that large rewards should go to those who offer dynamic leadership that may substantially improve the level of living of many people. At the same time, there is resistance to the idea that these rewards should be hoarded and passed on to heirs and successors. Society also needs a machinery for adjusting all incomes in relation to each other, with conflict and argument perhaps, so long as these are not disruptive.

The industrial battles fought over wage claims have a strange relationship to the unequal distribution of incomes. The fact that the highest incomes in society may range up to fifty or even a hundred times the median wage is not the kind of issue that gets seriously discussed. What worries a particular union is that its demand for an 8 per cent or 12 per cent increase in wages is met by an offer of say a 4 per cent or 5 per cent rise. There may be a dispute, therefore, over a difference of from 4 to 8 per cent. Or the dispute may be over demarcation lines between workers, and over the issue of who is eligible to join a union.

The question arises as to which kinds of differences in income are genuinely visible and which are not. Since the really well-to-do people in many countries spend their high incomes without deliberate ostentation, their high spending may cause little anxiety among the wage-earners. These, in their turn, worry more about the pay packet of the man next door. They resent a 10 per cent increase above their own level of someone whom they have regarded as their equal more than the 100 per cent rise in share values of their less immediate neighbour, who owns stocks. There is, as a result, a degree of phoneyness about the internecine struggles between unions, and between their official and unofficial leaders. The struggles are real enough, but they hardly relate to the extreme inequalities within the society.

These arise from substantial differences in earnings and also from differences due to property ownership and inheritance. Often earnings are easier to attack than other sources of income; so, for example, some developing countries have set limits on the earnings of top professional men like doctors or university professors, with an inhibitory effect on the supply.

The trouble with this approach is that there is a world market for professional services, and in any case there are alternative markets even within a country in which able men can sell their services. If doctors are offered too little at home they will work abroad, or adopt some form of 'moonlighting' to supplement their official incomes. A country roughly gets what it pays for, and where university teachers' salaries are set low, the teachers full-time tend to be inferior, and the abler ones work part-time in the university and make their careers elsewhere.

Similar difficulties arise if incomes of businessmen are kept artificially low, or if an attempt is made to tax away receipts from property. The only effective way to control inequalities arising from the skewed distribution of property ownership must surely be through a direct, or indirect, and through-going attack on ownership itself. The means are to hand in many countries for building up a considerable public-ownership share of manufacturing industry. This arises from the surpluses that often accrue for years on end from contributions to welfare funds. It is extraordinary that statesmen still seek to remedy the lot of the old age pensioner by adding to his fixed money claim. What private insurance companies offer with their 'with profits' policies is a share in the rise of equity values—if there is one. Given this tendency for long-term inflation, these values are more likely to rise than not. The huge surpluses arising in the welfare funds give modern governments a sound basis for entry to the same kinds of assets. Land is another outlet for long-term investment of funds.

The task of determining incomes from work fairly could be much assisted if incomes from property were to be tackled first. These incomes could easily become much more widely spread with a progressive pensions plan. Unfortunately there seems to be a rigid line of division between the kind of thinking that goes into government and private pension schemes. Governments tend to think only in terms of 'rights', and claims to fixed sums of money, yet the surpluses being built up in welfare funds throughout the world provide a ready means of financing the acquisition of assets, which would provide a hedge against inflation.

The determination of incomes could be more rational and fairer if the discussion was focused on grades. A systematic list

128

of grades in all industries should be agreed, and a set of minimum rates of pay for each of these grades negotiated. There would always be cases of earnings above the minimum, to be settled by direct negotiation.

The assumption underlying any idea of consensus, or of a rational solution to a social problem, is that there is some common purpose more or less acceptable to all members of a society. The well-known phenomenon of the unifying effect of a war with an external enemy is evidence of the need for this assumption.

In peace-time what is the unifying principle to be? Hume raised this question long ago, and Adam Smith answered it in terms of the 'invisible hand'. Each man by pursuing his own interests would, if competition prevailed, contribute best to the common good. The trouble with this argument is that there are so many exceptions to it. The simple pursuit of maximum personal gain will not contribute most to the wealth of the nation unless there are a number of restrictions laid down by the state. The Adam Smith recipe works well only if certain underlying conditions are artificially maintained.

The economist's ideal distribution of incomes tends to be based on Adam Smith—that distribution which would result from perfect competition being maintained in the labour market. Thus some economists criticize trade unions on the grounds that they create monopolies in particular labour markets; other economists praise trade unions on the grounds that they help to bring wages up to a true competitive level. What is common to both kinds of economist is the value judgment that the optimum wage level is that which results from a strict maintenance of competition.

Societies may choose other goals than that set by traditionally minded economists. However, if the attainment of some other goal involves a sacrifice or loss due to a departure from competition, this ought to be assessed and incurred deliberately, rather than inadvertently. Certainly, it would seem that incomes are determined by several factors, not all of which are consistent with a reign of competition.

A high variation of incomes within occupational groups seems

I

to indicate, where it exists, that competitive forces are at work, because individual workers are able to secure high wages owing to exceptional skill. However, the same phenomenon could be consistent with sets of non-competing groups and individuals, each setting its, or their, own price. Whether or not, in the long run, incomes are at or about the competitive level is the point that worries economists, but it may not be so important for society as the cost involved in getting incomes settled at all. There are the costs of strikes, lay-offs and go-slow campaigns, and there are the costs of raising taxes and transferring incomes so as to maintain some desired kinds of equality. These costs together may become very high. So may other indirect costs of wages being out of line with expectations, such as costs of high labour turnover rates.

A machinery that settles relative rates of pay without too much cost is desirable for its own sake. It seems difficult to imagine that any such machinery could be made to work if there were not simultaneously adopted by society some systematic programme for expropriating private owners of assets and placing an increasing amount of equity ownership in the hands of the community or its accredited agencies. Many societies already practice this policy more than they realize. Churches, colleges, cities and states acquire assets for social purposes and without a systematic plan. To extend this programme much more widely might be revolutionary in principle but it would not be novel.

It is not easy, of course, for anyone to decide what the public interest really is, either in general or in some particular context. In many instances the answer is difficult, and in some impossible, and judgment of a varying degree of arbitrariness has to be employed; had there not been this fundamental difficulty in socialism it would long ago have replaced capitalism—which frees many energies, but is based on the absurd premise that greed is a good thing.

Developing countries face the special dilemma that they are particularly ill-fitted to develop socialism, because they lack the social cadres from which efficient managers for nationalized industries could be drawn, and they lack the tradition and practice of skilled, sharp but urbane debate out of which a reasonable view of the public interest may emerge. In addition, they may be somewhat deficient in democratic governmental skills, although this deficiency can be made up in a few years by the newly educated classes. They may also be short of capitalist-style managerial talent. There are therefore peculiar difficulties, even for the impartial and beneficent onlooker, in suggesting which type of society would advance the economy best through its earlier stages. Apart from the objective problems of the situation, there are always many particular restraints imposed on each developing economy by its particular social structure, its distribution of land and of other resources, its historical relations with other countries and with world markets and by its political standing.

Despite these complications, there would seem to be some tendency for the world to have to move towards recognizably common patterns of income determination. The skills upon which economic growth depends are fairly mobile. The banking experts, economic planners, consulting engineers, oil-drilling technicians and farm-economics consultants move from one part of the world to the other with increasing ease and frequency. To organize the effective application of the skills of these experts involves more than merely consulting them. Nevertheless, the evolution of a world market in many skills has been marked in the last twenty years.

These experts not only tend to create some kind of common scale of reward for their own skills. Their very existence, and their capacity to undertake tours of duty in many parts of the world, creates the basis for comparing factor rewards at lower levels. For instance, it becomes apparent that, say, locally trained assistant civil engineers in country A are being given salaries much higher than those in neighbouring country B. Even though mobility of labour between countries is hampered by various barriers to visit or to migration, the spread of knowledge exercises a pressure and an effect, such as the well-known brain drain that occurs if developing countries fail to bring their rewards for their highly trained nationals up high enough to retain, or re-attract their services.

The studies of Professor Nove[1] and Dr Routh[2] suggest that the relative positions of industrial and other workers have changed in rather similar ways in Russia and Great Britain, over fairly long periods. Building, transport and industrial workers tended to improve their position relatively to the service industries between 1935 and 1964. Since then some skilled services like the doctors' and teachers' professions, have become better rewarded. In Soviet Russia, as in Britain, it seems that piece-rates and bonus payments have affected the comparative levels of earnings. Even where there is central control over wages and salaries, a certain degree of 'wage drift' is permitted, in response to labour market pressures. In the Soviet Union the authorities were able, apparently quite successfully, to prevent such 'drift' from upsetting the system, and to avoid an uncontrolled rise in wage costs. Nevertheless, such drift as took place affected industrial workers as against the 'staff' on their fixed salaries.

Relative skill differentials seem to have been falling in the long term in most economies. Mr Paul G. Keat's study provided data on 141 occupations in the United States from 1903 to 1956. However the results were weighted, they agreed in showing reduced dispersion between these two years. Another calculation for the United States estimated earnings per head in certain professions at two different dates (1904 and 1953)[3]. There was, in general, a distinct narrowing of differences between the earnings in the professions specified and the average wage in manufacturing, and between the professions themselves. University presidents and high school principals in 1903 received 7.75 times and 6·4 times the average wage, while at the later date they received only 4 times and double the average wage. Professors dropped from

[1] 'Wages in the Soviet Union: a comment on recently published statistics', by A. Nove, *British Journal of Industrial Relations*, Vol. IV, No. 2, July 1966.

[2] *Occupation and Pay in Great Britain, 1906-1960* by G. Routh, NIESA (Cambridge Univ. Press, 1965).

[3] Long-Run Changes in Occupational Wage Structure', by Paul G. Keat, *Journal of Political Economy*, 1960.

3·6 to 1·7 times that wage. Altogether there was no doubt that differentials had narrowed considerably.

It would be dangerous to jump to the conclusion that there is a general economic 'law', or persistent force, that results in a continuing resolution of differentials, and therefore in greater equality. Before World War II, there was some evidence that the wages-bill had been a fairly constant percentage of total national income, and whole theories (including a notable contribution from M. Kalecki) were invented to account for this supposed regularity. Later statistical work has thrown some doubt on the constancy itself. It would be rash now for us to guess that differentials will go on narrowing in future decades unless we have firm evidence that the underlying causes of past reductions are likely to continue.

There are forces working both ways. The new technologies that affect communications, data-processing and the storage of knowledge have two effects. Immense power will be within the grasp of those who have control of pivotal machines or processes. This would imply a strong factor working for greater specialization and a narrower oligarchy. Only the few, with brains that can use the machines, will be worthy of a 'top' position. But the huge economies of scale that can be obtained by mass production and distribution will raise the marginal productivity of many semi-skilled workers. Cheaper machines will diffuse some of these economic advantages.

Some sociologists have supposed that an objective assessment of the work content of each occupation may be made, resulting in acceptable differentials. In certain fairly well-integrated social environments, where communications are excellent, and assessors can be trusted—for instance, in a well-managed factory offering stable employment over a number of years—the 'objective' assessment may be workable. But society as a whole has unpredictable changes of demand and of applied techniques. The market for skills is subject to changing conditions like other markets. Is not the verdict of a competitive market usually acceptable? If electricians or carpenters are in short supply, they may for a while receive exceptionally high earnings, some gained by overtime. The equalizing force will be the increasing number who enter on courses to acquire the necessary skills. Public resentment is rightly directed against attempts to create monopolies of skills, or to restrict entry to given crafts or professions in an artificial manner, or for any other purpose than the maintenance of standards. But provided that entry is possible, temporarily high earnings for a skill are usually acceptable.

To hope than an agreed hierarchy of earnings can be imposed for all time is to pursue an ideal of stability that soon would become stagnation. A society so constituted would become saddled with a caste system, that would in the end impede social mobility. The determination of incomes must in dynamic societies always be a matter of getting market forces to work rather than of substituting bureaucratic decree for agreement. There have to be some institutional devices (such as social services) to offset hardships. But the market will give answers that no 'work content' study would confirm. Value, in a market system, lies in the eye of the purchaser, not in the judgment of the stop-watch assessor.

The social framework within which markets are encouraged to operate as freely as possible is not necessarily wholly permissive. Indeed, what is and what is not acceptable social behaviour has in recent years become very much one of the topics of open debate. Whatever answers are found to these questions, so long as legal and social boundaries are not crossed, producers of goods and services may offer what they will, and consumers value the goods produced and displayed according to their means and tastes.

The only other method of valuation is one where an authority is empowered to decide what shall and what shall not be produced. While, in certain circumstances such as a national emergency, this alternative method has clear net advantages, so soon as choice is enlarged the method loses relative merit. The socialist countries, as they get richer, run into more and more insoluble problems of valuation. Sooner or later, they make concessions to a market principle.

134

Acceptable inequalities are likely, therefore, in future society to be based largely on the idea of the market. The question asked will be not 'does he work hard enough to deserve that income?' but 'would he command such an income if competition were truly open?' So long as there is no suspicion of monopoly, and an income is paid that reflects the contribution of the earner's efforts to the market that he serves, the level of income is likely to be 'acceptable'. The incidental inequalities of receipts will not be challenged.

This situation will never be realized if there is not a visible effort made to expand opportunities for transfer between jobs and for the acquisition of skills. The rapid development, expansion and reform of educational institutions is therefore not a luxury, but an essential condition for societies with dynamic growth combined with some political stability.

CHAPTER 9

ACCEPTABLE INEQUALITY

There are only three possible outcomes—that equality and inequality remain much as they now are, that inequality gets more marked, or that it is reduced. Which is the most likely? And is one or other of these outcomes more favourable to human survival?

It would be difficult to prove that economic equality (however defined) was a necessary condition of social stability at any particular date, but it is difficult too to believe that greater equality is not a goal that human societies will continue to pursue. If this is so, there may be a limit to the frustrations that people will endure when some particular advance towards this goal is blocked. What has to be considered is the degree of inequality that different societies will find tolerable, or acceptable.

Societies may survive even when individuals or groups within them are discontented or rebellious. A number of pensioners, defrauded by inflation of the society's declared intention to maintain them in old age, may not for years constitute much of a threat to politicians in power, but with some change in circumstances the same degree of frustration may become critical by affecting marginal votes, or a political organizer may in some way crystallize the discontented persons into a moderately effective pressure group. A religious or racial minority may drive itself into some kind of social alienation that provokes precisely the kind of discrimination which it was ostensibly organized to combat. Some issue may arise, over school attendance or medical practice or anything at all, over which tempers are lost and even serious violence may break out. Long before looting and burning begin, symptoms of varying degrees of real or imagined inequalities appear. They not only have to be removed, but the alienated or ill-treated groups have to become sufficiently integrated with larger interests to lose their sense of differences and of discrimination. Often it is a privileged but threatened group which reacts violently against a proposal to equalize political or economic advantages.

Economic inequalities are only one aspect of all these problems but they are one real element in most of them. They provide a wonderful war-cry which stirs the guilty feelings of more prosperous peoples. So long as huge segments of human society remain so poor relatively as to be deprived of reasonable chances of competing for economic advancement, even individually, there will always be a good case for revolution. Moreover, there will be a continuing gross economic waste, since there is every reason to believe that the mute talents of the underprivileged will include abilities that, properly trained, could have benefited mankind.

The likely trends of change at present are twofold. First, as education spreads, as material standards of life even in the poor and heavily populated countries rise by a few points, there will be a movement towards an overall reduction in inequality, at least between full-time employed persons, but, secondly, as the pattern of human societies becomes more complex, and more and more based at key points upon the organization of advanced technologies, members of political and economic power groups will become more specialized, and their rewards in relation to the average will become more drastically distinguished.

Whether in mainly capitalist or mainly socialist countries, those who control the key decisions will constitute an élite. There will be an element of chance arbitrariness, certainly of injustice in the distribution of all kinds of material rewards in both types of society.

Among those in a position to choose today, some prefer the injustices of capitalism to the somewhat differently distributed injustices of socialism. The fact that in some respects both types of organization are changing towards a greater similarity of thought is not necessarily a step towards a society that promotes greater equality. The forces that make for inequality in both types of society are quite general, and likely to operate for some time to come. They are the need for incentives, to satisfy men and women of exceptional social and economic importance, and to meet what may sometimes be their more neurotic urges for power. Huge differences in power or wealth may sometimes be enjoyed vicariously. The fact seems to be that all societies look to ambitious people for some of their leadership, for some of their needed innovation and organization, and for some of their equally needed daydreams.

Indeed most societies recognize this, and as well as planning for greater equality they always reserve a place for inequality. 'Deserved' inequality, so to speak, although the principles upon which recognition of it is based may vary enormously from one society to another, is almost universal. The whole problem is essentially to design a working social institution that keeps inequality within bounds that are currently acceptable.

Neither the totally capitalistic nor the totally socialistic solution seems to be, even in principle, in the slightest degree capable of attaining such an end. The capitalist theory of 'dollar democracy' has the fatal flaw that the distribution of wealth and income which it permits (granted inheritance, compound interest, windfall profits to accumulators of land or capital and so on) has no relation to a rational system of incentives, and must end up with a distribution of resources skewed away from any possible ideal. Socialism attempts to remedy this by giving state institutions ownership of all land and productive resources, which reduces most inhabitants of a country to the level of wage-slaves of powerful bureaucrats, who, since liberal democracy is incompatible with such an economic system, must necessarily appoint themselves. Dollar graft is replaced by power graft.

The mixed economic systems that some societies are trying to operate must therefore reject capitalism and communism. They must use market forces, but never be afraid to challenge them. They must be prepared to use state enterprise, but always have checks and balances designed to control their bureaucracies. So far, probably no country in the world has found an even moder-

138

ately successful way of achieving this middle way, and, as few have clearly grasped the gravity of the problem, and the subtleties needed in its solution, this is hardly surprising.

The old bureaucracies have to go. The new ones will need to be as enterprising and energetic as, but more responsible than the old, so that the business leaders in the most successful economies of our time will be governed by equals. There are no universities yet fitted to train these people and no business schools yet designed to train their opposite numbers in industry. But, it may well be argued, the need for a constant pressure on leaders to take inequalities seriously and to alleviate them as they arise, is critical for survival.

Without fairly substantial changes in several important economies, it seems to be most likely that inequalities will grow rather rapidly. Modern technologies favour ever larger concentrations of economic and political power. Power, whether political or economic, is singularly blind to human feelings, even when it is benevolent in intent; money does not smell, as some empress once said, but neither does it feel very much.

The well-advertised cruelties that bureaucrats will inflict on huge populations in pursuit of some ideal society is matched on the capitalist side by the slums and labour camps, even by the sometimes well-appointed, but spiritually dead, company towns that ignore the waywardness of the human being. The division between the owners and the workers has not, with these institutions, been overcome—as a matter of fact it has hardly been ameliorated or its edges softened. The result sooner or later is a deadlock over some issue of incomes policy, or terms of employment, or something less relevant—in Japan it seems for some years to have been the American occupation of Okinawa.

The splits in societies and between societies can, of course, be ignored. This is perhaps more likely than any other outcome. For instance, the international aid programmes, which are based on unclear objectives and ambiguous phrases about 'take-offs', are likely to run into ever more acrimonious debates until they end up in undisguised charity, and unadulterated bribes handed out openly and cynically to hangers-on and political supporters. The power struggle between nation states dictates this conclusion. The breakthrough to an international society that seriously tackles inequality problems will surely only come when the existing social order is threatened. This will not necessarily come only with civil disturbance, war or open violence, but may arrive as a result of drastic economic pressures, such as are now operating to change Europe's political structure.

The poorer countries are very large, and many of them are populous as well as growing rapidly in numbers.

Wholesale famine is not inevitable, since advances in agricultural technology, such as the introduction of hybrid strains of cereals and the wider use of fertilizers, as recent Indian experience has shown, are in principle able to meet the rising demand for food. If local famines occur they will be symptomatic of a breakdown in distribution. But these large poor countries can provide markets for, as well as resources essential to, the more industrialized societies. Sooner or later this basic fact must change the attitude of the richer countries from one of indifference—a reaction from imperialist involvement—to one of serious and active participation.

The scale of this involvement has to be immense. This is not a question of a few thousand experts or a few hundred Colombo-plan students, but of several million persons involved in annual interchanges. It is a question of ending racial and religious estrangements, and modifying centuries-old taboos.

As people are not even aware of this need, although they know of its technological feasibility, they still build their national, regional and suburban fences and defences. But they are gravely at fault if they think that this can be more successful than Canute's command to the sea. The international inequalities are of an order that involves most nations in drastic and rapid change. These international involvements will not be helpful in relation to domestic inequalities.

Great movements of peoples will be taking place within national boundaries as economies in all continents develop, but they will spill over the national boundaries. The orthodox view that because emigration cannot solve the population problems of rapidly growing countries, therefore no significant migrations need take place internationally, is going to prove to have been shallow. The Indians who went to Fiji, South Africa or the Caribbean, did not travel to solve an abstract 'population problem' at home but simply to better their individual condition from one point of view or another. The same need to change places of residence applies to Greeks, Spaniards, Turks and to many Asian peoples, and the motivation will get stronger not weaker.

Inequality of rewards attracts flows of people, even according to orthodox static economics. The great laws of simple economics tend to work, even though legislation and conservative societies seek to impede their operation wholesale. The need for labour in the northern countries of Europe has led to the huge influxes of immigrants despite the 'we do not want them' attitude of sections of organized workers in all the relevant countries. When the forces of inequality build up a sufficient potential, the resistances are overcome.

All that needs to be said is that, in this changing world, to work hard for an acceptable degree of inequality—or an acceptable approximation to equality—will be not just an idealist's ambition but a necessity for survival. So far, in the European countries slight modifications of inequality seem to have been attained. The migrations have been fairly successfully handled. In the developing countries, and in the world as an international unit, inequality has probably been getting a great deal more marked.

The need for international and national bodies to keep these sources of social friction within bounds is immense. This is not just a question of banning for ever a few criminals and multimillionaires, but of ensuring that acceptable ranges of salaries be adopted for numerous occupations and skills, of making transfer between countries easier for all, and of restraining great accumulations of private wealth by world-wide agreements on taxation and fiscal policy. These policies are never likely to be universally successful or even universally tried. But they may be quite widely adhered to, if they prove to have some social value. The controlled capitalism of the future has so much to offer the world that a 'mixed' system may continue to evolve in most of the advanced and advancing countries. Even if not universally applied, some of the drive for greater equality must be realized in some countries, based on a realistic acceptance of a rewards system that promotes social change and advancement.

What has to be faced is the fact that international aid schemes on the one hand, and progressive taxes on income or capital gains on the other, have not provided the answer to the social need for equalization programmes. International aid, so far as non-communist countries are concerned, reached a peak of some $11 billions in the mid 1960s and seems now to be in decline. It may recover to a higher level in the 1970s, but there is little evidence to suggest that its magnitude will grow under present arrangements and motivations by any really significant amount. The developing countries were growing at best at some 2 per cent per head per year in the early 1960s—say at about $2 a head in countries with some $100 of national income—while the growth of the developed countries was many times this figure (about 3·7 per cent on a much higher base). For a large family an extra $2 a head would not be negligible, but the comparative rates would not mean a narrowing of the gap between the poor and rich countries. The trouble is that even the aid rate of the past seems to be difficult to maintain.

Within advanced countries, taxation systems aimed at diminishing inequality have begun to be counter-balanced by inflation of equities, whether in business or private assets or land, by tax evasion and avoidance, and by a movement of the very rich to domiciles in low tax economies. Unless powerful social forces begin to operate, the forces of inertia seem more likely to increase than to diminish inequalities.

What could such powerful forces be? The periods of diminishing inequality in the industrialized societies have coincided with wars and their aftermaths, which in economic terms means periods of labour shortage. World Wars I and II both made heavy demands on manpower. Mass armies and navies had to be mobilized, and huge complexes created in a short while to service modern industries designed to promote wilful destruction. After the wars were over, many nations still needed an influx of manpower, to rebuild industrial capacity and to work it, to provide the labour force necessary for economic growth, and to replace the gaps in the middle age groups that had suffered the heavier casualties.

When this mobilization—and labour utilization—programme was being actively pursued, labour as such gained a stronger bargaining position. The evidence of the historical studies of wage and earned income differentials suggests that these periods of intensively high demand for labour diminished inequalities and that this effect persisted for a number of years. If this broad interpretation is right, the question becomes: can any similar rise in the demand for labour be anticipated as likely to arise without another tragic war, with its implications of loss of life, destruction of property, and threats to continued rational social existence.

Sometimes it would seem that no such future is even possible, let alone probable. The essence of technological advance is often seen to be in labour saving devices being invented and promoted. But many new technologies are capital saving as well as labour saving. Each new economic advance, moreover, has in practice—and in direct contradiction to the wooden predictions of some professional pessimists—been accompanied by large increases in the total absorption of labour.

Thus the United States in the 1950s and 1960s, the EEC countries, the United Kingdom, Canada, Australia and Japan all required immigrants on an unexpectedly large scale to meet their labour requirements. The effect of increasing automation has so far been not, as the dismal jeremiahs foretold, to give rise to secular unemployment, but rather to increase the opportunities of many families to raise their purchasing-power. As this has expanded, so has the demand for labour in many dozen occupations, and the end of this increasing demand is not yet in sight. Is there any reason to suppose that this trend will soon be reversed? On the contrary, there are in most advanced countries still a host of service industries to be developed and expanded (in transport, tourism, education, health and many other activities). Most of these industries depend upon individual employees willing to specialize in learning skilled and semi-skilled trades.

The unforeseen demand for labour in the developed countries has been met by immigration into these countries from some expected and some unexpected places—Greeks and Spaniards can be found concentrated in the car industry in Melbourne, Turks in Düsseldorf, Pakistanis in Bradford, and so on. These people, the migrants, themselves represent an equalizing process at work that acts across the dual problem of disparities of income within and between countries. The likelihood of a rising demand for labour persisting into the future depends upon what view one takes of human behaviour and economies of scale. Are wants initially insatiable, and have economies of scale (and of specialization) yet been fully exhausted? If the answer to the first of these questions is a qualified affirmative, and to the second negative, a continuing pressure on labour is likely to persist.

Any equalizing tendency that this situation may create needs to be strengthened by an adequate redistribution of asset ownership, or else it will be offset by the opposite tendency for the rich to get richer. Once a certain surplus can be accumulated by an individual, he may build his savings up by the effects of compound interest, but still more of capital appreciation. This accrues to him directly or indirectly as a consequence of the development of the whole society. Not only land values, but mineral values, or equities held in industry, may advance in value as a result of the community's growth. Those who have some surpluses at the critical moments will reap investment returns that may easily offset any trend towards equalization in earnings.

The conclusion must be that greater equalization of incomes is not impossible to imagine, but that it may be partial, affecting only some sectors of society, and leaving behind it a certain dualism between the rich and the poor. If this is indeed the outcome, countries with a strong democratic condition and system will become impatient with authority.

To the extent that a social goal of greater equality is desirable, how far should any country go i n seeking to attain it? What costs should it reasonably incur?

Gross and rising inequality is not the only threat to the social order. Stagnation is as big a danger as revolution. Economies dominated by wealthy patricians or plutocrats with large inherited interests are not usually anxious to accelerate any kind of change. This is not an argument for abolishing distinctions of wealth, but it does suggest a need to bring inequality down to a working level, an acceptable level.

What may be acceptable in a country like Sweden may be very different from what is acceptable in, say, Italy and still more different from what passes in an oil sheikhdom in the Persian Gulf. It is not to be expected that all international differences can be ironed out or that there is much to be gained by attempting such a Herculean task. But to make the world both a more manageable and a faster-growing place it has been the contention of this book that inequalities between and within countries must be reduced to an acceptable level. Even this limited objective. varying as it must from place to place, demands programmes of a drastic and radical kind. Some would label them revolutionary, as indeed they must be in the sense of demanding a considerable upheaval of many existing economic and social institutions.

In this essay, no overt treatment has been given of the political implications of such a programme; clearly much research work has to be done to establish how closely political upheavals of a violent kind are usually related to economic grievances and inequalities. The hope may be expressed that revolution, in the special sense of total overthrow of existing regimes by violence, is not a necessary stage towards the kind of necessary modernization of society that this study has been written to support. Certainly some violent revolutionary outbreaks may occur. They may even, in some countries at some stages of development, contribute (though at a cost) to the ultimate reduction in that country of its pattern of inequality. The trouble is that the consequences of a revolution, and particularly the timing of these consequences, are extremely unpredictable. A society ruptured by a breakdown in government rarely ends up with a pattern of behaviour anywhere near the pattern which its internal critics had tentatively formulated. A revolution does not necessarily lead to a reform—it may, and often does, lead to a counter-revolution.

While it would be naïve not to face the logical necessity of some complete changes in the behaviour pattern of nations, if an acceptable level of equality is to be achieved, this study is not intended to point the path to achievement, but rather to stimulate discussion, in various local contexts, of the validity of the goal.

INDEX OF NAMES